"What a delight to hold in your h
of God who loves and lives the '
work that will relate to people fro.   y .....s of ....e. want
to be touched by heaven? Read this book!"

Dr. James Goll, founder, Encounters Network,
Prayer Storm and GET eSchool;
author, *The Seer*, *The Lifestyle of a Prophet*,
Praying for Israel's Destiny and many more

"This is truly a remarkable book. God shows up supernaturally in the life of a helpless, emotionally wounded and
scarred child; also to adults who are completely sold out to
the Lordship of Jesus Christ. He will become more alive and
real to you as you follow Nancy on her fascinating, enlight-
ening journey."

Mrs. Joy Dawson, international Bible teacher
and bestselling author

"*Touched by Heaven* by Nancy Ravenhill is captivating and
kept my attention from the moment I began to read it. I
found myself not wanting to put it down. The book had me
teary-eyed at times, especially in regard to her earthly father.
At one point I had to put the book down, and went to my
preteen daughter to remind her of how very much she is
loved, valued and cherished. Nancy, with such vulnerability,
candor and honesty, shows us the amazing grace, redemption
and healing of God for our lives—even through the crucibles
of our experiences. Her stories are not only inspiring, but
deeply heart touching and a constant reminder to us of the
reality of the manifest presence and destiny of God. I personally was reminded of my own life journey, and the divine
encounters and landmarks with Jesus along the way. This

book will bring life and raise a renewed expectation in the Lord and His providential plans for each of us."

Doug Stringer, founder and president,
Turning Point Ministries International,
Somebody Cares International

"Rare is the book that balances supernatural experiences with the ebb and flow of living life on earth, especially during the times when life seems to be harsh and severe. I highly recommend Nancy Ravenhill's book, *Touched by Heaven*. No matter where you are in life, there is always hope that God and all He has created is there to help you."

John Paul Jackson,
Streams Ministries International

TOUCHED BY
HEAVEN

TOUCHED BY
HEAVEN

Inspiring True Stories of One Woman's
Lifelong Encounters with Jesus

NANCY RAVENHILL

Chosen
a division of Baker Publishing Group
Minneapolis, Minnesota

Published by Chosen Books
11400 Hampshire Avenue South
Bloomington, Minnesota 55438
www.chosenbooks.com

Chosen Books is a division of
Baker Publishing Group, Grand Rapids, Michigan

Printed in the United States of America

Library of Congress Cataloging-in-Publication Data is on file at the Library of Congress, Washington, DC.

ISBN 978-0-8007-9604-4

Unless otherwise indicated, Scripture quotations are from the New American Standard Bible®, copyright © 1960, 1962, 1963, 1968, 1971, 1972, 1973, 1975, 1977, 1995 by The Lockman Foundation. Used by permission.

Scripture quotations identified ASV are from the American Standard Version of the Bible.

Scripture quotations identified ESV are from The Holy Bible, English Standard Version® (ESV®), copyright © 2001 by Crossway, a publishing ministry of Good News Publishers. Used by permission. All rights reserved. ESV Text Edition: 2007

Scripture quotations identified MESSAGE are from *The Message* by Eugene H. Peterson, copyright © 1993, 1994, 1995, 2000, 2001, 2002. Used by permission of NavPress Publishing Group. All rights reserved.

Scripture quotations identified NKJV are from the New King James Version. Copyright © 1982 by Thomas Nelson, Inc. Used by permission. All rights reserved.

Scripture quotations identified NLT are from the *Holy Bible*, New Living Translation, copyright © 1996, 2004, 2007 by Tyndale House Foundation. Used by permission of Tyndale House Publishers, Inc., Carol Stream, Illinois 60188. All rights reserved.

Scripture quotations identified PHILLIPS are from The New Testament in Modern English, revised edition—J. B. Phillips, translator. © J. B. Phillips 1958, 1960, 1972. Used by permission of Macmillan Publishing Co., Inc.

Scripture quotations identified KJV are from the King James Version of the Bible.

Cover design by Dual Identity

15 16 17 18 19 20 21   7 6 5 4 3 2 1

To the Praise and Glory of God, my Father, and Jesus Christ who gave His life for me and called me to fulfill His purpose that I might serve Him with love in His Kingdom. I thank Him for guiding me to David, my wonderful husband, and for giving us our three beautiful daughters, whom we named Lisa, Tina and Debra; our very special treasures. "For with God nothing shall be impossible."

Luke 1:37 KJV

I waited patiently for the LORD; and He inclined to me and heard my cry. He brought me up out of the pit of destruction, out of the miry clay, and He set my feet upon a rock making my footsteps firm. He put a new song in my mouth, a song of praise to our God.

Psalm 40:1–3

CONTENTS

Contents

FOREWORD

Reality television is showing us that we love to learn about real people and their daily lives. Everyone loves a good story, especially a true story.

The incidents you are about to read are true. What is even more important is that they happened to someone just like you. My good friend Nancy Ravenhill has been a Christian longer than I have been alive. In this book, she opens her heart to share some trials and triumphs, and lets us see the extraordinary ways Jesus has revealed Himself to her from her childhood to the present.

While we might not have the exact same experiences as Nancy, we should all expect God to reveal Himself to us as the great I AM. My prayer is that as you read about these encounters with Jesus, you will come to experience the touch of heaven in your own life. Remember, He is the same yesterday, today and forever; He will never stop being who He is—the supernatural God!

Mike Bickle,
International House of Prayer of Kansas City

PREFACE

Every person I know has a life story to tell! I find it fascinating to listen to people talk about their lives. The past is always interesting, the present can be daunting—but we look to the future with eyes of hope and expectation, by faith.

My story begins when I was five years old, and my life changed dramatically. I could not imagine how I would walk through the difficult days that were to come. But the Lord Jesus Christ had compassion and love for me, and so began a journey with God that I never expected. I began to know Jesus as my true Father and found Him in my heart. I learned that we see Jesus most clearly in the hard times—when we cannot make it unless He helps us.

The supernatural experiences God has given me have quickened my spirit and shown me how very real, dear and near our heavenly Father can be. I never forget Jesus' divine visits, His amazing appearances, His voice to me and, most of all, His face.

It was in Christchurch, New Zealand, in 1981 when the Lord came to me on a beautiful sunny afternoon and told me, *You're going to have to write a book about your life one day!*

I turned around abruptly and said, "Lord, I'll never do it. I don't want anyone to know about my life." I said no, but I knew that day that this assignment, the writing of God's visits to me, would be completed by His grace.

That day has come. I pray that you will be blessed, encouraged and quickened by God inside your heart as you read and live these stories with me. In the words of the beautiful hymn,

> Yesterday, today, forever, Jesus is the same,
> All may change, but Jesus, never—
> glory to His name! . . .
> All may change, but Jesus, never—
> glory to His name!

Nancy Ravenhill
Siloam Springs, Arkansas

ACKNOWLEDGMENTS

Recently, while in a small village in Turkey, my husband and I watched a young girl weaving a carpet on a loom. Above her hung numerous colorful threads that had to be carefully selected and then tediously, skillfully, strategically placed and knotted by hand in order to produce a true authentic Turkish carpet. We were told that a large carpet could take more than a year to complete.

Without Ann McMath Weinheimer's skill, patience and ability, my book would never have been enjoyable and readable. While I supplied Ann with the various threads of my life, she wove them into an accurate account of my experiences. Ann, it was a pleasure and privilege to work with you. I can truly say that without you, this book never would have been written. Thank you so much!

I also want to thank my husband, David, for his much needed wisdom and help, as well as his willingness to write the epilogue.

My thanks also to Jane Campbell, who began this journey with me and encouraged me to the end.

Finally my thanks to Linda Valen, who was the first to suggest that I contact Jane at Chosen Books. Linda believed that my experiences should be told and that they were worthy of being published.

Above all, my thanks to my wonderful Lord. To Him be all the glory.

1

THE STORM BREAKS

And he shall be like the light of the morning when the sun rises, a morning without clouds, like the tender grass springing out of the earth, by clear shining after rain.

2 Samuel 23:4 NKJV

I walked timidly into our living room, curling my small finger along the pink flowers in the wallpaper and making my way quietly to the big chair beside the picture window. Our house was a short walk from the shores of Lake Michigan. On this day, the late afternoon sun streamed through giant puffs of clouds onto her dark waters.

My parents did not seem to notice me. They stood facing each other, feet planted, eyes locked. Their voices were almost indistinct in the shrill and uncontrolled effort to be heard one above the other.

I had listened to these same words and angry sounds many times in the past few months. Like those other times, I climbed up into the thick arms of the green flowered chair, drew up my legs and crunched myself into the cushions. I felt particularly inconspicuous that day in my pink and green plaid shorts, my long brown hair pulled back into braids. I am not sure why I was drawn to be close to them. Seeing them filled with anger made me desperately sad, but still I came. Not making a sound, I peeked out from my garden of fabric leaves and blossoms.

My mother took a deep breath and, pointing her finger in the air, spoke with deliberation. "If you would get a steady job, we wouldn't always have to be worried about money."

My father, who had begun pacing, stopped long enough to glare in her direction. My father was not tall, and they were nearly at eye level. "I could get plenty of jobs," he said, his voice like a growl. "But we'd have to move and you won't give up your teaching. You're just working to make me look bad—to make me look like a bad provider!"

"That's not true, Billy! You know that I only went back to work so that I could earn a living. Nancy has to have the proper things." My mother's voice faltered for a second, then took up her charge: "I have to pay for her to get through a good school. And she needs the right clothes to wear in the right places. You aren't working," she added, "so somebody has to."

Her accusing tone must have hit a nerve. "That sounds so noble," my father shouted. "You spend money to dress up a five-year-old. I suppose what I want doesn't matter!"

At the sound of my name I had instinctively drawn back. It felt like an unfortunate intrusion into an adult world that

I did not understand. The arguments about money were unending; yet money seemed always to be available. My mother did her best to improve our humble surroundings. She bought beautiful things with her teacher's salary—our matching "mother-daughter" dresses from Marshall Field's, the marvelous department store just around the lake in Chicago, my new bedroom furniture, and even a piano so that I could take lessons.

And Daddy *did* work. I loved to hear him play his pearly black and white accordion. At least, he wanted to work. He had given up his nightclub jobs, and requests were not plentiful for a Christian accordionist; nor, when found, did they pay well.

So, they argued. Words like *mission field* and *service to God* were part of Daddy's new vocabulary now that he was saved and we were attending the Baptist church. He wanted passionately to become a missionary—and dreamed of returning to the Caribbean to live. The previous summer a church there had paid for him to come and minister, and he longed to return, for they loved both his accordion music and his preaching.

But his appeals fell on deaf ears. My mother, also newly converted, was determined to keep her job with the Michigan school system to provide "the proper things" for me, which meant that he was stuck in St. Joseph. Was money the problem, then? I wondered. Or was I really the problem?

The dark and sudden rumble of thunder that was Daddy's voice startled me. I had not moved an inch toward the storm, but neither could I move away from it. It turned on me with fury.

"This is Nancy's fault!" Daddy roared.

With two strides he was standing in front of me. He reached down and grabbed my upper arm, pulling me out of my chair, and steered me roughly into a corner. With my father before me, I was now flanked by two windows on the attending walls—the large picture window on one, and a high side window up near the ceiling on the other. There was no place to hide, nowhere to go; the corner seemed, rather, to hold me prisoner under two watchful, silent eyes.

"This is Nancy's fault!" he bellowed again. "And she's going to find out what it's like!"

I watched his hands twitch with furious motion as he unclasped his brown leather belt and pulled it quickly through the loops of his trousers. I had never been hit before and did not know what he was doing. Then with his arm drawn fully back and leaning the weight of his body into the blow, he ripped the leather across my legs.

The jolt shot through me like electricity, burning my flesh and numbing my brain. Stunned, I managed to lift my arms to cover my head.

"You are going to learn!" he shouted, berating me with every blow to my torso and bare legs.

I bit my lip till it nearly bled, fearful of making a sound, sensing that cries would enliven his rage. Yet I could not help wincing each time he raised his arm. I squeezed my eyes shut to block out the vision of the next explosive strike.

Eight . . . ten blows. . . . My legs were going numb and my body was beginning to sway.

Then at last, when I felt as though I might crumple to the floor, the booming thunder ceased and the earth grew still again. I opened my eyes and lowered my arms. Daddy was breathing hard and putting his belt back through his pant loops. After cinching the strap through the buckle, he turned with a kind of swagger and faced my mother.

I looked between them, from his lifted chin and searing eyes to her shocked silence. Neither looked at me. Neither offered me help. Slowly I put one foot in front of the other and walked painfully past them, past my silent garden chair, up the gray carpeted stairs and into my bedroom, where I collapsed onto my knees at the side of my bed.

My little room, normally so cheerful with its pastel stripes, was a blur as my eyes flooded with tears. Sobs shook me uncontrollably; I buried my face in the bedspread to muffle the sound.

Two things were clear to me, young as I was. One of them I had suspected, but it was painful to comprehend: I was utterly helpless in a violent world. I sensed, correctly as it turned out, that this was not the sole incidence of my father's brutality. In part because of my mother's non-interference, his rage at her had found an outlet. Their only child had become a mute sacrifice to brutal passion.

The other thing clear to me was that I had only one place to go. I marvel at this comprehension, but it was true. In all the world I knew that no one could help me; no one would believe me—even assuming I could lift the veil of shame and tell; no one would walk with me through the terror.

No one, that is, but Jesus.

Through watery eyes, wiping my nose with the back of my hand, I looked up at the picture of Jesus that hung on my wall. It was a painting of Jesus in a garden, surrounded by three children. Under the painting was written a question that the children were asking: "What happened to Your hand?" I would often lie in bed at night, look up at that painting and long to be one of those children. They were safe there with Jesus. He would help them.

But I was not one of those children. My days were destined to be sad and lonely, stretching out past any hope I might try to envision on the horizon. I was not even like the other children in my Sunday school class. As of that day, I was the caretaker of a terrible dark secret: the shattering rejection of my parents. I was numb with the insecurity and pain that reality brought me, and wondered how I would make it through the rest of my life. Who would take care of me and guide me as I grew up?

But still I knew, somehow, that the answer to my hurt would be found in Jesus. One of the Bible verses we had learned in Sunday school was a promise from Him: "Lo, I am with you alway, even unto the end of the world." I loved to hear my mother quote those poetic words from the King James Version to me. "Lo, I am with you alway. . . ." I clung to the hope that those words were true, that He was somehow with me as the Bible said.

Filled with loneliness, barely able to whisper, I mouthed syllables of a prayer to the One who was the only answer to my broken heart. I told Him about the good changes I had seen in my father. I explained that I did not know what I had done to provoke such a whipping. Even as I spoke those words, though, I knew that I was not really to blame. Not really. I told God that He was the only One I could trust, and the only One who could help me.

After some time, I tried to calm down. I had stopped hoping that I would hear a kindly step on the stair. I glanced sadly at the door, then more positively around the room. The ceiling slanted down on one side, meeting the yellow, pink and green striped wallpaper that rose halfway up the wall. This was a wonderful feature, for it felt closed-in and protective. Two little windows on the opposite wall looked out over the redbrick street.

Then, my eyes were caught by movement—something appearing. . . . Was it possible? I scrunched my face to focus more clearly. Yes, there stood a man in a white robe! Incredibly, I had no doubt that what I was seeing was real. And then I knew, somehow, that God had heard my prayers. Not only that, the true living God had come to help me and was standing in the corner of my room.

I was not afraid, and looked at Him steadily. I had learned about the Trinity at church and wondered which Person this one might be—the Father? the Son? the Holy Spirit?

As He looked down at me I sensed in my innermost being that this was Jesus. He had brown hair touching His shoulders, and His face was serious, but kind. His whole presence was serene and quiet. In my amazement, the tears slowly stopped spilling out of my eyes.

Though He wore a robe, He looked very natural. I had seen Sallman's famous *Head of Christ*, everywhere present in churches and Christian homes, and I thought how He resembled the depiction offered in that gentle brown painting.

With Jesus there, I was in no hurry to get up from the side of my bed. I watched Him for what seemed like ten or so minutes. Then I looked away for a second, and when I looked back He was gone.

I had never heard anyone say that Jesus would come and visit this way, but at that moment, His love went deep into my soul. I could not comprehend how the Lord could be there with me, or even how I could sense the Spirit of God, but one thing was clear: Jesus was with me, and I was His. The Holy Spirit had filled my room. I wanted to live for Jesus the rest of my life.

Another thought rose in my mind, equally difficult to comprehend: What would His presence in my heart mean for me? What difference would it make in my world of arguments and isolation and pain?

That day as I knelt by my bed, battered and bruised, I did not know the answer. Both of my parents had shattered any hope of the world as a secure place. I was in a tiny boat on the vast sea, with turbulent and angry waters threatening to drown me. I could do nothing on my own to reach the safety of shore. How would Jesus help me navigate through the overwhelming feelings of rejection and worthlessness?

Perhaps you, like me, learned early in life that pain is not a one-time experience. If so, then I want you to know this truth: God is with you as you walk out the hard times, the times you cannot make it unless He helps you.

I could not imagine it that afternoon as I knelt on the floor, but God was going to allow me to taste the powers of the world to come. Jesus would appear to me multiple times on earth and in eternity—and He would even show me the second heaven, the realm where evil resides.

Why? So that I could know in my own heart and share with you that the supernatural is very real. Help is at the ready from heaven for you and for me.

Jesus does not have to appear physically to do that—although sometimes He does! God even answers our requests to see more visibly into the supernatural realm. We cannot force a vision to occur, but we can walk in deep intimacy with Jesus so that experiencing the supernatural is the natural outcome. More and more, people all over the world are finding this to be true. Jesus is always with us, and we see Him most clearly in the difficult times.

The Bible says, "Your own ears will hear him. Right behind you a voice will say, 'This is the way you should go,' whether to the right or to the left" (Isaiah 30:21 NLT). As you become attuned to the supernatural in your own life, you will see that the world to come is the *real* world.

Heaven exists—and it can touch your life.

2

DEMONS
IN THE SECOND HEAVEN

And what shall I more say? For the time will fail me if I tell of [those who] from weakness were made strong [and] turned to flight armies of aliens.

Hebrews 11:32–34 ASV

Days and then weeks passed from that experience of seeing Jesus, and I wondered if the dark cloud might lift from our home.

I had learned not to stay around my father too much, and certainly not to irritate him. Even when I tried to help him, he would rebuff me. I longed for him to care about me, but my attempts at affection—once I offered a timid kiss on his cheek—were not returned. I cannot remember any time that he showed me real love.

Sometimes he would sit me in a chair and practice preaching. Though I was careful not to swing my legs and held my hands clenched together in my lap, I did learn much about the Bible. Other times he would lift his heavy accordion to his chest and play beautifully the hymns that we sang at church or a complicated classical piece. His desire to be on the mission field with his accordion consumed him.

One night, like any other, I listened to my parents argue. Mother had come home tired from teaching school all day. Daddy had cooked supper and generally kept house. Though he loved to cook, he always looked frustrated with this arrangement. He would grumble once again that he could get a good job if we moved, but she was adamant.

To make things worse, she kept emphasizing how dependent we were on her income. They had lived in rented rooms for years; this was the first home they had owned. Once a month, he left the house saying that he was going to go pay the mortgage, and she paid for the food and car and utilities—and splurged on me. I knew that finances stirred up his anger and kept them in a tug of war.

Daddy had a round face and dark hair—in fact, he had had aspirations of becoming an actor, but parts never materialized; he was always scowling and looking irritated. Sometimes darkness would come over him. This night, I was to see that evil with new eyes.

Their voices escalated and I was not able to slip away to my room in time. I gasped as he grabbed my arm roughly and pushed me into the corner. I watched, shaking and mute, as he took off his belt, and the blows began. This time my mother wept, but once again she did not come to my rescue.

I hung my head and took it. When finally his fury was spent, I slowly made my way up to the sanctuary of my room. Their arguing resumed, but I shut my door and the bedroom walls blocked their voices. As I knelt slowly and painfully by the side of my bed, the only sound evident was my sobbing.

I cannot explain how I knew at age six that the change in my heart when Jesus appeared to me some months earlier was real. I see now that I stood at a crossroads this night, and that my future would be shaped in part by how I responded to the pain. There on my knees, I responded in a way that, I believe, opened the door to receiving His ministry through the supernatural.

That action was simply to cry out to the Lord with my whole heart and soul.

It is possible that I got this concept of bringing my pain to Jesus through a godly pastor and his wife who would come and have Bible studies with my parents, praying and weeping before Jesus long into the night. They pastored a Church of God congregation in the Midwest, and their kind and gentle natures modeled what I thought true servants of God must be. There was a little register in my parents' bedroom floor that they could open, allowing heat to rise up from the living room below. Whenever this couple came I could peer through the grate and actually watch their prayer meetings.

So now I turned to Jesus with every ounce of my being. I did not look anywhere else for solace—not in toys or a book or a distraction or anger or any other person. I talked to Him straight.

"You are real, Lord Jesus," I said, "and I am going to come to You with my whole heart." I held nothing back. I told Him that I felt cheated by the way my parents treated me, and how they did not care about me.

Taking a breath, I said through my tears, "Lord Jesus, my father doesn't drink or smoke now, but he is mean to me. I don't like my parents anymore. I don't know what to do. Please help me."

I did not see Him this time, but knew He was there. The presence of the Lord was all around me.

Then, quietly and quickly, I felt myself going up into the atmosphere. I thought that every part of me had gone up into a heavenly place, but I realized later that my body had remained beside my bed. I hung suspended in midair. Even though I could not see Jesus, I knew He was there.

"Where am I?" I asked.

This is where Satan and his demons live.

"But where am I?"

This is the second heaven, He said. *This is the place I gave them where they live and work.*

Everything moved around me in slow motion. I was not afraid because I was with Jesus. I did not look back to see my physical body on the floor, and I never looked down to see what this spiritual body looked like. I still felt like "me." I simply stood there in midair, looking at whatever came in front of me.

Odd creatures glided slowly in the distance, and then one or two would slide toward me, floating around me. They were grotesque beings that I never could have imagined. One or two looked as if their bodies were box-shaped—either rectangular or square. One was like a pyramid. The boxes looked to me like cardboard—white, gray and silver, all subdued colors. Their heads and necks stuck out of the boxes, as did little legs. Even their hair was grotesque. It stuck out like matted straw from a gray scarecrow, dry and stiff, and covered the tops of their heads.

They looked like combinations of part animal, part human. Some had tails stretching out but eyes that looked human. Some had scales. I knew they were alive.

These days, on television and in movies, demonic beings are readily visualized. But that was not the case when I was a child. I had never seen anything like these creatures.

They moved close enough for me to see them clearly. They projected evil. At least twenty of these beings wafted around me, circling and looking back at me.

They stayed a good six feet away; a boundary separated us. I think the Lord was telling certain ones to come, as He was controlling everything. They were not scaring me. It seemed as if they knew they were being told just to let me see them. They did not make faces or talk to me.

As I said, I was not afraid. I was just observing. And all this time I knew I was not in heaven, but up in the atmosphere, which amazed me. There was quietness and peace because Jesus was there. Although Satan did not come into view, I knew it was his realm.

Then the Lord took me back. I was just suddenly back in my body by my bed after what seemed to be three or four minutes.

Jesus wanted to teach me something through this, but what was it? Clearly, He wanted me to see this realm and understand it, but what effect would this aspect of the supernatural have on me? If these beings were real, and I had no doubt they were, did they have influence on my life? It made sense to me that they did. It made sense because the feeling I got from them was the same feeling I got from my father when he was so angry and thrashing out.

And that, I realized, was the point. I think that Jesus was showing me that this was the reason my dad was the way he was: He was being harassed by these demons. When he began arguing with my mother and got so frustrated, these evil beings came into the house—the blackness, the darkness.

I had the sense that the teachers in our church would not endorse the conclusions I was coming to. They did not believe that a Christian had anything to do with the demonic realm. You "got it all" when you were born again—salvation, deliverance. Everything was taken care of.

But my dad was disproving that doctrine for me. When he was born again, he changed in many good ways. Overnight he stopped drinking, smoking and swearing. He read Scripture and got up in the early hours to pray. He even got on his knees and wept. Still, darkness would come over him, and he would not resist it. He would shout at my mother and whip me brutally. I think a spirit came on him—or in him. He needed deliverance.

It was sobering to think of this demonic realm, of such evil. But that is what I think God wanted me to understand—that I was facing darkness.

And you are, too.

Nothing I have experienced throughout my life has caused me to doubt this. These beings are real. They target us, driven to earth full speed ahead at the behest of Satan as his ambassadors. They are not slacking off at any point in plotting our destruction.

How do they operate? Demons, I believe, are allowed to whisper to us, to attack our minds. They seem to be trained to break down the Body of Christ. Their goal is to grip hearts for an eternity in hell.

But we can resist them and their evil power. How grateful we can be for the blood of Jesus Christ! Through His death and resurrection, Jesus conquered evil and death, and when we belong to Him we need not fear.

You and I are spiritual beings. If there is a presence of evil, we will sense it—and God expects us to resist it. The outcome for us in times of attack, then, can be determined in great part by how we respond.

By God's mercy that day, my response was a good one: I turned to Jesus. I did not focus on the demonic.

Nor over the years have I focused on any one-two-three system for combating evil. Jesus will show us how to follow Him whenever the enemy tries to distract us by fear or pain. Still, there are a few biblical principles that can help us keep our eyes on Jesus as we walk through the hard times when it seems as though evil will win.

If you are under attack, the first thing to do is to *get on your knees and pray with everything you have.* Be hungry for Jesus' presence. I think that suffering actually does this for us—it increases our hunger. If things are occurring in your life that you cannot deal with, that you do not have an answer for, realize that it is only the living God who can help. The enemy will often send confusion to distract our minds from looking to Jesus. Rebuke the darkness that you feel, whatever is overwhelming you.

The next thing is to *realize that you are not alone.* So many people in the world today feel lost. They have no one who really loves and cares about them. There is Someone who cares, and He will never leave you.

Then, *pray the blood of Christ over that situation.* That is all we have. The blood of Jesus protects us from all demonic activity when we avail ourselves of the armor the Lord has provided for us to wear (see Ephesians 6:11–18).

Finally, *give Jesus the glory.* He is the victor.

We need to remember that Jesus defeated the enemy, Satan, through His work on the cross. Colossians 2:15 says: "He stripped all the spiritual tyrants in the universe of their sham authority at the Cross and marched them naked through the streets" (MESSAGE). The Phillips version says: "Having drawn the sting of all the powers ranged against us, He exposed them, shattered, empty and defeated, in His final glorious triumphant act!"

Let me give you an example of how this looks. This incident might seem like a little thing, but it shows how the enemy wants to disrupt even the smallest details of our lives.

The other day, after visiting a shopping mall near our home to pick up a few things I needed, I went out into the parking lot and, my head down against the blustery wind, walked toward my car.

That, at least, was my intention. The car was nowhere in sight. I looked up and down the rows of vehicles, certain I had left it in that section. I gripped my packages more tightly as the wind blew me along. I never lose my car; this was absolute confusion. Soon I was certain that someone must have stolen it. I simply could not find it.

I made my way back to a bench outside the entrance door and sat down. I knew I had to anchor my heart in Jesus. Composing myself, I got my keys out—which were not electronic, so I could not flash the lights on the car—and prayed to the One who is always with me. I told Him that I was distraught—that I could not see the car. "I belong to You," I said. "You have to help me."

I rebuked the confusion I felt. I continued praying and asking for God's peace, and peace came. I got up and began walking again. This time it did not take more than a minute to locate my car once the confusion had gone.

The enemy is ready to attack at any moment. That is why it is particularly important not to open any doors for him to gain access into our lives. Some of these choices include certain television shows, movies, books or music. Demons can gain entrance through these things. Paul warned the believers in Ephesus not to "give place to the devil" (Ephesians 4:27 NKJV). Any sense of conviction from the Holy Spirit that we should not look at something or go somewhere should cause us to listen and obey.

As 1 Corinthians 6:19–20 says, we are not our own:

> Do you not know that your body is a temple of the Holy Spirit who is in you, whom you have from God, and that you are not your own? For you have been bought with a price: therefore glorify God in your body.

Why, then, if God is in charge, do His people suffer at the hands of evil? All I can say is that God had a plan for my life—and He has a plan for yours. When we have nowhere else to turn, we can believe that Jesus will help us. He is always there. We can trust Him.

The Bible says that the heroes of the faith "from weakness were made strong" (Hebrews 11:34 ASV). Second Corinthians 12:10 says that the same is true for us: "I am well content with weaknesses, with insults, with distresses, with persecutions, with difficulties, for Christ's sake; for when I am weak, then I am strong."

Granted, I had a long way to go toward understanding. These thoughts were just beginning to form that night when Jesus took me to the second heaven and showed me the power of evil affecting our home. In fact, the next time I sensed His presence with me, I turned away in unbelief, never thinking that God would be concerned about my world of pain and disappointment.

3

SEEING IS NOT
ALWAYS BELIEVING

For He Himself knows our frame; He is mindful that we are but dust. As for man, his days are like grass; as a flower of the field, so he flourishes. When the wind has passed over it, it is no more, and its place acknowledges it no longer. But the loving-kindness of the LORD is from everlasting to everlasting on those who fear Him, and His righteousness to children's children.

Psalm 103:14–17

When my father and my mother forsake me, then the LORD will take me up.

Psalm 27:10 KJV

The days labored their way through another year. No one knew what was happening in our house. We never talked about how much screaming, crying and arguing occurred week after week, or how unhappy we really were. I was afraid to tell anyone about the terrible whippings. I did not want the world to know that my parents had rejected me, so I kept it a secret. I hoped that if I never mentioned it, people might love me—or at least think well of me.

I was also afraid to tell anyone about the extraordinary experiences I had in the presence of Jesus. In the first place—and this was true about the whippings as well—I was sure that no one would believe me. People would say I was making it up.

Our Baptist church taught that all supernatural activity ended with the apostles. I mentioned that our congregation did not believe that Christians could be harassed by demons. Nor did it expect to be particularly blessed by God. There were no more healings, no more special giftings from the Holy Spirit and certainly no more visitations from Jesus. As far as our church was concerned, the book of Acts tells of special events that happened two thousand years ago—not today. My father believed this quite strongly. The supernatural, in his mind, simply did not exist.

Our pastor was deeply loved, a wonderful man with a kind heart. One Sunday morning as I was leaving church, he leaned down and put his hands around my face.

"Are you okay?" he asked.

My eyes filled with tears, and I nodded. That was the most I ever acknowledged to anybody during those long, painful years.

On Thursday afternoons after children's choir practice, he would drive many of the children home in his car. He always asked me if I wanted to "make the long trip with him," meaning he would take me home last, and I always said yes. He would tune in Bible stories on the radio for me to listen to as he drove me back to my house.

His compassion—and perhaps understanding—touched me. Still, week after week our congregation nodded its assent that the book of Acts was closed—and any supernatural manifestations with it. This unyielding teaching, and the fact that I was terrified of crossing my father, shrouded the light of understanding that was beginning to dawn in my heart. There was no one to talk to. Though I was naturally outgoing, I grew quiet. My voice got softer, out of fear of projecting myself.

There were rays of hope. I remember going to Washington School the first day after a new year began. Our teacher, Mrs. Norris, was a pretty young woman, cheerful and friendly, and we kids loved her.

The first day back after Christmas vacation, just before my eighth birthday, Mrs. Norris wrote *1950* on the blackboard in large figures. She began to talk about a new year ahead of us, as well as a new decade. That day stood out in my mind—the possibility of newness, and what that might look like.

My mother was working at Washington School, teaching the first grade. I could see her classroom on my way out to recess twice a day. Often she was standing at her door talking with her students as I passed by. She always smiled and said, "Hi, Nancy." At school she talked to me just as she did the other children, maintaining a professional demeanor.

At home, I felt that she tried to value me. I remember asking her during bath times, "Mommy, why do I get birthmarks?" It never occurred to me that the black and blue marks that came and went on all parts of my body were from my father's belt. No one ever mentioned the bruises, perhaps because I was so freckly all over. She never answered my question, but watched me as I washed myself in the tub. I remember, though, looking up into her face, and it was sad.

Mostly my mother expressed her sympathy for me through new clothes. "Nancy needs to have nice things," she would tell my father. I was always, as the old folks used to say, dressed to the nines. I remember a beautiful blue tweed coat I wore to church. It was perfectly fitted and had a little collar with dark blue piping around the edge.

Nobody had clothes such as I had. Once I counted 57 dresses in my closet. Two or three of these dresses were part of our "mother/daughter" sets. Before I was born, Mother—who went by the nickname "Bunny"—had been a model for a department store in St. Joseph. Her hair had turned white when she was just in her twenties. With her young, attractive face and trim figure, she was quite striking.

I saw even then that the dresses were her way of trying to make things up to me. But material gifts could not relieve the emptiness. And spending money on me only fueled the fire of my father's temper—money was being wasted on me that could help him reach his dream.

I lived my life with my friends. I longed for a brother or sister to play with me, but as the years went by I realized I would be an only child. Most weekends found me with my grandparents. We were very close through these years. They were a gift to me from God.

After school each day I walked the few blocks home, and prayed that the nights would be peaceful. They rarely were.

One school night, not long after the new decade had begun, my father began shouting about the extravagances of my clothes and hit me hard with his belt. I was finally released, and walked past him and my mother, crying quietly.

What had I done to deserve this? There was no good answer to that question. I never knew what triggered his wrath, except that I provided an outlet for his frustration. I think he also enjoyed upsetting my mother; in many ways she instigated his pain. She usually cried as she watched him.

I climbed the stairs slowly that night and fell to my knees by the side of my bed. After praying, telling God everything in my heart, I got undressed and crawled under the covers. I listened for my mother to come up and tuck me in and read a Bible story, as she did most every night, but I knew better: She did not come to my room any night that I was whipped.

I lay still, staring at nothing in particular.

Then I realized that someone was standing in the corner— opposite to the corner where I had seen Jesus before. I could not see Him, but I could feel His presence. I looked around.

"Who, honestly, are You?" I asked out loud. Deep, deep down in the warmth of my heart I knew that it was Jesus Christ. But how could Jesus be making Himself known to me? All the adults in my world denied that possibility.

Then I heard Jesus' voice speak to me audibly. He said, *I'm going to visit you all through your lifetime.*

At first I was struck with the comfort of the Presence behind the voice. I absolutely knew that a Man who had lived forever was standing in the corner of my bedroom. When He spoke, however, He was closer to me. He had moved toward me. His presence was powerful. Something very solid, very strong, almost massive had come into the room. Just as powerful was the impact of beauty, peace, great love. I did not see Him with my physical eyes, but my heart thudded with wonder.

He was pouring out love, but my thoughts swirled down into confusion and anger. I was being tormented, chastised for things I had not done when my father whipped me and my mother seldom attended to me.

I wish I could say that I responded with faith and trust to His wonderful words, but the truth is I did not. I reacted without thinking. I directed my hurt toward Jesus, denying His words of promise that He would visit me throughout my life.

I said, "Oh, God would never do that for me."

I could sense His presence for a full minute, maybe longer. But I turned off my light, rolled over and closed my eyes.

The atmosphere of my room changed as He left. I fell asleep almost instantly. I will never forget sleeping so soundly that night after hearing the voice of the Lord. And the next day and the next I wondered about that peaceful sleep after speaking those rebellious words.

Really, I knew that it was Jesus coming to me. Even though I felt insignificant and unimportant, I knew that God was always with me. I tended to see His light most clearly in the darkness of the lowest valley. His presence was in my bedroom that night, and in my pain He gave an amazing promise to me.

Why did I reject it? I have wished a hundred times afterward that I had accepted His word to me. But even though I rejected Him, He did not reject *me*! He loved me with the comfort of His presence even when I turned away.

God is so creative. Nothing is impossible with Him. When we hunger and thirst for Him, He will give us divine embraces—whatever form that might take. It does not mean that we will always see Him with our eyes or feel the warmth of His arms, though many people have seen Him visually down through the centuries—and some of those individuals painted pictures of Him as they saw Him.

Actually, I think that He appears differently to people. When He appeared to me in these early times, He was a little older than you might expect, fuller in the face—a more fatherly appearance. This was perhaps His way of helping me be comfortable with Him, since He was actually fathering me. Who knows? Who can outguess God?

There is nothing too hard for Him to accomplish. Even when we doubt and have fear, He can encourage and help us. The supernatural is a way that He works in this world—and the Holy Spirit stirs our hearts to believe it can happen.

Still, we often miss it. Or, as I did that night, we *dismiss* it. How many times has the Holy Spirit revealed to us the presence of Jesus, or gifted us so that we might grow in Him and help the world understand more about the Savior—and we reject Him? How many times has Jesus spoken to our hearts and we do not believe?

Probably many. But that is not the end: God works with us knowing where we are.

Because I did not agree with God that night, I think I missed an opportunity for Him to impart something to me. I believe He could have touched me and brought healing into my life. I was eight years old on this memorable night, and I did not believe Him—but He did not give up on me! He did not condemn me; He did not leave me. He found other ways to reach down and help me.

Even though I spurned His promise, I still clung to the truth that the only way out of my life was to keep on praying; so I continued to pray. I grew up keeping quiet through the years of whippings, but always crying out to Jesus by the side of my bed. I had no place to go other than the Person of Jesus Christ.

He knows how to help us through our mistakes. He can get us where He wants us to be. Ultimately, I think that you and I wind up right on schedule. He always loves us, always works toward our good. Scripture says that even "if we are faithless, He remains faithful; He cannot deny Himself" (2 Timothy 2:13 NKJV). And look at these comforting words: "He knows our frame" (Psalm 103:14 NKJV).

One thought kept my feet trudging along the path that rose up and out of my dark valley: *Without Jesus I will never make it*. He guided me with the promise of hope.

Times of doubt and unbelief are not the end. We can let our hearts trust even when we cannot see. We can let Jesus help us. He will never stop trying.

4

A VISION FOR THE FUTURE

Then the LORD answered me and said: "Write the vision and make it plain on tablets, that he may run who reads it. For the vision is yet for an appointed time; but at the end it will speak, and it will not lie. Though it tarries, wait for it; because it will surely come, it will not tarry."

Habakkuk 2:2–3 NKJV

My mother came upstairs and read Bible stories to me almost every night—except, as I mentioned, for the nights I was whipped. She would pull *Egermeier's Bible Story Book* from my little white bookcase, and sit on the other twin bed.

We would talk about the day together and everything that happened, and then she would pray with me. I was always in bed, ready when she came. She seemed to enjoy these times together. Often while she was reading the Bible stories, I would look at the painting of Jesus on my wall—the one of Jesus in the garden with the three children. These bedtime stories provided special times with my mother.

I spent many hours reading the books she bought me. One was named *Flight of the Silver Bird*. It was a large blue book, and it told the story of two children who flew with their parents down to the southern hemisphere. They slept overnight on the plane in small beds. I read this book over and over, wondering what Australia and New Zealand must be like. Never did I dream that one day I, too, would fly to those wonderful places.

The years passed, and I began to grow up. I studied hard at school and found the most comfort reading and studying my Bible. After my father whipped me, I would turn to its pages. I was still getting hit quite a lot. I had no confidence. I was so ashamed of my life.

One night when I was twelve years old, I was going up the stairs to get ready for bed when my mother called out, "Nancy, wait." She got up from her chair in the living room, where my father continued to sit silently.

She came up behind me and put her hands on my shoulders. I continued walking slowly, step by step, up the gray carpeted stairway as she followed me. This was unusual in itself, but when we got to the landing at the top of the stairs, she stayed behind me with her hands on my shoulders. Then she said, "Nancy, let's pray for your future husband tonight."

Those words embarrassed me, so certain was I that no one would ever love me after all the whippings I had endured. And I despaired over the brown freckles that covered my face and arms and legs. I would look at other girls in my junior high school and think that I was the ugliest person in St. Joseph. But I bowed my head dutifully and closed my eyes.

As she began to speak, a clear picture appeared in front of me. I lifted my head, keeping my eyes shut. A huge, beautifully colored map of Europe was spread out before me. I recognized England and Ireland, Holland and France, all in various pastel colors.

I heard the Lord call my name clearly. He said, *Nancy, you will never marry an American. You will marry someone from this part of the world.*

He kept talking to me, saying that all my friends would go on to college, but that I would go to a special school, one I had never heard of. He told me that He would arrange everything and get me to the school He wanted me to go to.

Do not worry about anything, He said, *because I will take care of you and cause this to happen.* He was telling me this in a fatherly way, a tone I never heard from my earthly father.

Just as my mother finished praying, the Lord stopped talking to me, and the vision melted away.

I opened my eyes and looked at my mother but did not tell her what had happened. I was mute. I kissed her good-night, and retreated into my room wondering about this experience.

Was this possible? Hope for the future?

My heart was racing. God, the living God, had come to me and spoken a wonderful promise.

But how could it ever be? There was no money for college. And marriage? That thought ricocheted from the sublime to the ridiculous. I longed for physical beauty, but felt overweight and ugly. I ached for acceptance, but did not feel good enough. I tried to act like everyone else, but it was just a game I played. I felt terribly alone.

Still, something had transpired in my heart: Once again He had placed His promise there. Now I had a choice to make.

Since it would be impossible to accomplish anything close to that on my own, and since there was no hope for anything good apart from His gracious touch, then perhaps I could simply say thank you, and wait to see what He would do.

About a year later, I was nearly asleep one night when I felt His presence in my room. It truly seemed as if the Lord was standing at the side of my bed. I began to speak to Him, even though I could not see Him.

I told God about my fears and then, mustering courage, added, "Lord, if I ever do marry, I would like to marry a minister. And please, please give me a beautiful name. I am so tired of the name Schultz! There are so many people in this town that have that name. It goes on, page after page, in the phonebook." I turned my head into my pillow and went to sleep, not comprehending how God could give me a husband—or a beautiful name.

This promise often came to mind, but ultimately weakness and fear overtook me. My father made his rejection of me clear, and my mother was absent emotionally and mentally.

So I focused on trying to make friends and doing well in school. I studied the Bible with a passion. The words in 1 Corinthians 1:27 assured me that those who are weakest have the advantage of recognizing their great need for Him: "God has chosen the foolish things of the world to put to shame the wise, and God has chosen the weak things of the world to put to shame the things which are mighty" (NKJV).

I loved the Youth for Christ Club at school and the Bible Quiz Team. Even though I often knew the correct answer, I was afraid to speak out, afraid that I would make a mistake.

The whippings continued until I was fourteen, and then gradually stopped. Hope arose that there might finally be some normalcy in my life, but when I turned sixteen, my mother had a heart attack and nearly died. Her left side was paralyzed. She had more to do than she could handle in life, and it broke her. When she got out of the hospital and we knew she would live, Daddy seemed to mend his ways a little and act more compassionately toward her. He still seemed irritated and unhappy, though, and was not easy to live with.

My junior year in high school, he announced that he had made a decision. He said simply, "We're moving."

I had just a month left before the end of the school year, but he took me out of school and told me that we were going to California immediately to be near some relatives. He said that he had sold our home and much of our furniture. I had to quit my job at "Murphy's five and dime" downtown, and say good-bye with hugs and many tears to my beloved Grandma and Grandpa, as well as aunts, uncles and cousins. It was traumatic for me; I did not know if I would see any of these relatives ever again.

Daddy decided to take a few pieces of furniture with us and some other things we would need, so he bought a small trailer to pull behind our car. One rainy day, before I could comprehend what was happening, I crawled, silently, into the crowded backseat, and Daddy started the engine.

Just as he began to ease our overloaded car and trailer into motion, he put his foot on the brake, and we all took one last look at our home in St. Joseph. Then my father turned to my mother, who looked weak and frail. With a slight grin playing at his mouth he said, "You thought I was going downtown to pay the mortgage every month. I wasn't. I was only paying the interest."

It was a moment before Mother could speak. "You mean all these years you never paid the mortgage? I thought the house was debt free."

He laughed and released the brake.

I felt chills up and down my back as I thought, *You have lied to us for twelve years!* I was sick in my heart as I remembered his words, spoken often, telling my mother he had made the mortgage payment.

The fear of God came into my heart that day. As we drove away, I promised myself that I would never lie to anyone, especially my husband, if God ever allowed me to marry. My father's words made a huge impact on me; I understood instantly the damage that comes from lies. His words at that moment challenged me always to tell the truth.

We spent the next three months in the Los Angeles area near family. Daddy decided to move north to a tiny place in the Mojave Desert called Adelanto.

The high desert was the driest, most barren place I could imagine on earth. A cousin gave my father a small piece of land, with mountains in the far distance, and he set out to build a house. All the California relatives gathered one weekend on that spot and put up the frame—and then left the rest for us to finish.

Miraculously, the sale of our home in St. Joseph covered the cost of building the little house, but we could not afford anything extra. The floor of my bedroom was cold gray cement, but I had a small throw rug between my twin beds. There was no money for shoes or dresses in my size. From a boatload of clothes in Michigan, I now had little that was wearable. There was barely money even for shampoo or soap. But we had a new roof over our heads and, somehow, we had made it through another fragile year.

I started my senior year in the fall. Because there was a Youth for Christ Club at Victor Valley High School, I was able to find a place to fit in. By the grace of God, I made good Christian friends that year. In music class, two other girls and I formed a trio. Soon we were singing at the Youth for Christ meetings and rallies. Before I knew it, I was traveling almost every weekend with other students who sang, played their instruments and testified about their love for the Lord.

Oddly enough, God had reversed ministry roles between my father and me. Though I was not being paid, still I was the one traveling to meetings where I could sing and timidly give my testimony. Even though Daddy spoke at some churches on weekends, generally he would sit at home, looking depressed as I left the house. I did have the feeling, though, that our family's financial needs drew him to his knees in prayer.

My senior year ended, but I could not find a job anywhere. I had hoped to earn money for college. Sometimes I would look out our front door and see nothing but miles of sand. My future looked equally barren.

As college began that fall for all my friends, I turned to the Lord, weeping before Him as I remembered the promise He had given me of a "special school." I did not know what to do but pray.

After about two weeks, my father said to me, "Get in the car. We're going to take you to Biola College and talk to someone there." He and my mother felt that there might be some financial aid available since he was doing his best in full-time ministry. While certain that this was not the school God had mentioned, I did not argue. I put on one of my ill-fitting dresses and got into the car.

When we arrived at La Mirada, where the new campus was located, my parents asked to see someone in charge and were directed to the Dean of Men's office. I sat in a waiting room. Finally, the dean came to the door and asked me to come in. He looked at me kindly and said, "Nancy, we're looking for people like you."

I could hardly believe my ears. He offered me a scholarship to pay for my college classes, saying that he could arrange for me to work in an office at the May Company in downtown Los Angeles to help cover the expenses of my room and books.

He picked up the phone, and in a few minutes everything was arranged. He then handed me a meal ticket to use at the school cafeteria. I was utterly stunned. God had put the whole thing together. Granted, at the time it did not make sense to me. I knew this was not the school God had told me about, but this was a miracle, and I needed to take this next step.

We rode home to the high desert, retrieved my few belongings, and turned right around to drive back to Los Angeles.

As my father and mother were about to leave, I felt a great sense of fear about the future. How would I walk through the days ahead? My father turned to me and held out two twenty-dollar bills, saying, "Keep this money for emergencies, Nancy." But before the day was over, I had given every penny I had to buy textbooks.

Classes had been in session for two weeks, so there was catching up to do, but I was now a student on a scholarship, with a part-time job in an office downtown. Each night after dinner, I ran up to my room (I did not have a roommate), and spent time first in prayer by the side of my bed. I prayed to God, asking for assurance that He was with me. At midnight,

I turned out the light from my studies, and set the clock for five a.m. so I could catch the bus that took the Los Angeles students out to classes at La Mirada.

Although I tried to feel assurance that my heavenly Father was taking care of me, my bleak financial circumstances were embarrassing. The other students proved to be a great group of kids, and no one was demeaning, but I noticed how they chatted and laughed together so confidently.

I had no dates with the boys—I was overweight and felt that I was not good enough. Sometimes on Saturday nights, I climbed the stairs to the top story of our dorm, and watched the girls walk out to meet their dates and get into their cars. They could not see me up there in the window, tears pouring out of my eyes.

I realized as the months went by that the Lord was using that season for me to learn to walk by faith. It was a time of intimacy with Him. It was humbling—but strengthening. Psalm 138:6 told me: "Though the LORD is on high, yet He regards the lowly" (NKJV); I had nothing to boast about. Proverbs 3:21–23 assured me: "Keep sound wisdom. . . . Then you will walk safely in your way" (NKJV); in the aloneness of my life, He was all I had.

I clearly could not make it unless He helped me.

One night, by the side of my bed, I asked God what to do. Hours of homework awaited me, and I was tired before I began. Besides that, my few dresses were threadbare, and I needed certain supplies for my classes.

I began pondering this verse: "I, the LORD, search the heart, I test the mind, even to give to each man according to his ways, according to the results of his deeds" (Jeremiah 17:10). Something like a sword went through my heart. In plenty or in lack, He was asking the same of me: Would I be faithful and devoted? Was He really first in my life?

As I prayed, the sound of wind rushed into my room through the window behind me. It was the presence of the Lord, amazing and awesome. I began to weep uncontrollably. The Holy Spirit was breaking my heart over that verse. I stretched out my body on the vinyl floor, sobbing as God lingered above me, bodily, near the ceiling of my room.

He spoke to me: *Will you give up your degree?*

This surprised me. My mind had become adjusted over the months to the idea of a college degree so that I could get a good job. Through sobs, I gathered the courage to answer Him with a question: "Lord, how will I get through life? My mother had to teach school all of her lifetime."

Then He turned, and the wind and the presence of the Lord left slowly through the window as He said to me, *Someone will take care of you all through your lifetime.*

The reality of this supernatural experience was overwhelming. But I knew the voice of my Lord, my Savior and my God, and that His promises were true. I continued to weep and to worship Him, not realizing that I would transfer the next fall to a Bible school in Bloomington, Minnesota. It would be at that "special school" that I would meet my future husband, a young man with a calling from God to be in the ministry, who had a very beautiful name.

5

WHO WERE THOSE PEOPLE?

Do not neglect to show hospitality to strangers, for thereby some have entertained angels unawares.

Hebrews 13:2 ESV

In the meantime, I had school bills to pay, so I kept my job through the summer. Three other girls from Biola were in the same position, so we rented an apartment together in Los Angeles. It was a walk of several blocks to and from the May Company every day; this saved bus fare. I saved every quarter. Even though I had a scholarship, my school bills were huge.

One hot day as I headed down the street to work, I passed a man who was holding a small bundle of tracts. He thrust one of the pamphlets into my hand. Certain that it was a religious tract, I said politely, "Oh, I don't need this. I go to Bible school." But he was insistent, so I nodded, took it and kept walking.

I began reading, bumping into one person after another on the crowded sidewalk. The title was *We Need Men Aflame*. I had never heard anything like it. The author talked about the Holy Spirit coming like tongues of fire on the Day of Pentecost, and how we believers can experience today the same outpouring and gifting described in the book of Acts.

The idea that the Holy Spirit could fill you and that you could be endued with power was entrancing. I longed for "more," but had no idea how to get it.

After reading every word, I said out loud, "Whatever this man has, I don't have it!" All I knew to do at that point was slip the tract into the book I had brought to read on my coffee break, and later I put it into my box of special things.

I was able to visit my parents a couple of times that summer when a ride was available. The popular interstate Route 66 was visible from their house. People they knew traveled through occasionally.

One weekend, a businessman offered me a ride. He talked the entire trip about how much my parents needed me, and how lonely they were. He told me that I should come home to live and get a job in order to help them financially.

He was prodding me like a pitchfork, but I just let him talk. He was not listening to God, and I knew to ignore this. In the first place, my parents had money to live on, both in a savings account and from an inheritance my father received when one of his brothers died. But, in the second place, I knew that my calling was elsewhere. There was no point in explaining anything about my life to this man; he was focused on making me feel guilty, but I had no guilt in my heart.

So when we finally arrived in Adelanto, I thanked him and found someone else to take me back to L.A.

Knowing Jesus and drawing close to Him made the difference during those long months. Our hearts and minds can get confused by all the choices in front of us—and our choices determine where we go. Even though I could not imagine how the promises He had given me would ever bloom into reality, I was able to keep them in the sunshine at that point in my life.

When I walked into my parents' house, the first thing I noticed was that my piano was gone. I loved to play the piano; it helped to pass the hours there. My mother told me that she had sold it to get money to buy her new false teeth.

Their home remained a lonely place. My dad argued with me much of the time, but I promised my mother to come whenever possible in order to spend time with her.

The next time I went up to the desert to see them was toward the end of the summer. I walked into the house, and before I even sat down my mother handed me a college catalog. "You must read this," she said. "The woman who stayed here said you must."

"Where did you get this?" I asked. Then I heard the amazing story.

One evening at about dusk, they heard a knock at the door. Standing there was a nice-looking young couple who said they were missionaries traveling through. They said they had been told that they could get a room for the night at this house.

My mother said that this perplexed her, as they never had guests stay overnight. But she thought to say, "Well, our daughter is at school and not here right now. You could use her room tonight."

The couple thanked her and stepped into the living room, where they began talking almost nonstop. They said that they used to be professional dancers, but now were attending a Bible school in Minnesota. They were preparing to be missionaries, and had come to California to raise money for their future work.

My father got out the Bible that night, and they had a time of study together—something that my parents loved to do.

The next morning, they all had breakfast and another wonderful time together. Before the couple left the house, the young woman handed my mother a catalog from Bethany College of Missions, part of Bethany Fellowship in Bloomington, Minnesota. She said, with a touch of sternness, "Make sure your daughter reads this catalog the next time she comes home." Then they left.

What an unusual couple! Mother and Daddy had problems getting along with even their closest friends, so this tension-free visit made an immediate impression on me.

I took the catalog from my mother's hand and opened it. I knew instantly that this was the "special school" the Lord had told me about when I was twelve years old! It was the one that would point me in the right direction.

The pages were filled with photos of the school, and described everything that took place there—the office areas, girls singing in trios, the classrooms, the church, people working in the print shop, people building trailers, people strolling around the beautiful campus.

My heart was leaping. I looked at my parents, who were watching me, and said quietly, "This is the school I must go to."

My father spoke up right away. "Nancy, if you finish paying off your school debts at Biola, I'll pay for your train ticket to go to Minnesota and you can attend this school."

Truthfully, his offer to pay for my ticket surprised me, but then I realized that he did not want to take care of me any longer. He had told me so a year earlier. I think he figured that if he paid that ticket, I would be gone. Then, perhaps ensuring his release of me, he said that he would pay the three hundred dollars for tuition as well.

My mother knew I could not afford financially to go back to Biola for another year, and she also knew that I was being stretched to the limit physically. She did not say one word.

So I agreed to his proposal. I would study at Bethany for three years in preparation for the mission field. My future was planned quickly and decisively. I wrote Bethany College of Missions, requesting student-application forms.

Back in Los Angeles, I told my friends simply that I was transferring to a Bible school in Minnesota. They were all happy for me.

Incredibly, my acceptance came almost immediately. Before I left Los Angeles—my debt finally paid off—my friends surprised me one night with bags and boxes of wonderful things. They gave me a gray wool skirt, a red sweater, a yellow bathrobe and a black dress to wear on Sundays.

Their kindness and sensitivity toward my need overwhelmed me. We all hugged and said good-bye.

Thus, within two weeks of my last visit home I was boarding a train with my suitcase and heading to Bible college.

The train ride from California to Minnesota took three full days. When the other travelers took their meals in the dining car, I stayed in my seat and nibbled from the box of food I had packed for the trip.

The first day, a beautiful teenage girl sat next to me. She was a high school student returning to Minneapolis. She told me that she had become pregnant and that her parents had sent her off to California to give birth. She had given the baby up for adoption and was now coming home to begin her life over again. With many tears she told me the details of her story.

I shared with her about the Lord Jesus, and she gave her heart to Him. I saw her once after that. She brought her parents to Bethany to see me about a year later. I felt that she was trying to live for the Lord, but had no one to help her. All I could do was pray for her.

The last day before arriving at the Minneapolis train station, I decided to cut my hair. For missionary life I needed everything to be "easy care." I took a pair of scissors from my purse and went into the ladies' room. About fifteen minutes later I emerged as a new person with a new mission.

I loved Bethany from the first moment. This was home.

I made every effort to find the young couple who had visited my parents, but was told repeatedly that no students, past or present, fit that description. I was left to wonder.

As I mentioned, tuition for three years of Bible school was only three hundred dollars plus a job assignment on campus. The administration asked simply that you be serious about entering the mission field. Students were trained in practical, biblical and spiritual matters in preparation for service.

My mother had told me that she and Daddy would send the tuition as soon as I arrived, so I had to sign up for classes on faith. The administration graciously allowed me to begin my studies, but still the three hundred dollars did not arrive.

It was embarrassing; tuition was so cheap and mine was not paid. I called home many times asking them please to send the money. I realized later that they were waiting for interest to accrue on the money my father had inherited. I have no idea why they did not tell me this up front. Finally, though, after about a month, they must have acquiesced to my pleas because the money arrived. I do not know how I kept going; I only know that God had promised to walk with me through the hard days.

Once the financial obligation was met, school life became a wonderful whirl of classes, new friends, work duty—and the ability finally to lose weight. Whenever my clothes got too big, I rummaged through the missionary barrel in the school's laundry room and found something to wear. Sometimes I was asked to sing a solo at the church on campus, so I would visit the missionary barrel again. The Lord provided wonderfully, but I always wondered who was in the audience looking at me while I wore the clothes she had given away!

Mostly I learned about prayer. The editor of *DaySpring* magazine, on staff at the college, was a well-known British evangelist and author by the name of Leonard Ravenhill. Bethany was so much like a family that, in most cases, the students called staff members by their first names. I learned all about how the Lord had led Leonard and his wife, Martha, and their three sons to come from England and to settle at Bethany Fellowship. One of my friends was dating their middle son, David, a shy young man in my class.

Leonard's primary ministry was not speaking, although he was a superb speaker. His primary ministry was prayer. He prayed many hours a day. Then, when he spoke at Bethany Missionary Church, as well as churches around the world, the Holy Spirit would come down upon him and grip hearts to follow Jesus more passionately.

I was overwhelmed when this great man of God spoke. I often remained in the pew after the meetings while the others filed out; I could not leave. I stayed and pondered what God had just given us through His Spirit. I also began to go down to the church in the evenings around nine o'clock at night. Leonard would be there, praying with students who knelt at benches in the prayer room behind the auditorium. Anyone was allowed to come. I could never gather the courage to pray out loud, even though I longed to.

The year passed, and I kept studying, working and singing. Then one day, David called me and asked me for a date. Though I knew that he and my friend were no longer dating, David and I hardly ever spoke in class, so I was surprised. But I accepted. We went to a circus and had a good time. When he brought me back to campus, and we sat talking quietly, I realized that we would always be together.

After we had dated for eighteen months, he asked me to marry him. I was thrilled, and knew in my heart that he was the right man for me. Still, one afternoon I went into my closet—a literal prayer closet with a small window. I looked up into the brightness of the afternoon sun pouring through and asked the Lord if this was the right thing for me to do. I had to be absolutely sure.

Just then, my little box filled with my special things caught my eye. I had not opened that box in three years. I lifted the lid, and there on top was the tract handed to me that hot day on the street in Los Angeles. I picked it up and read it again.

Everything the tract talked about had come to pass in my own life while at Bethany. I had experienced the baptism with the Holy Spirit, as well as understanding and experiencing His spiritual gifts while there.

I turned the tract over and read these words at the top: *By the British evangelist Leonard Ravenhill.* I lowered the tract slowly, leaning my back against the closet wall. I could hardly believe my eyes as I read the name of the author.

Here was confirmation that the two promises given to me in my childhood had been fulfilled: He had brought me to the "special school" and had led me to the man I would marry.

My heart overflowed with wonder and amazement as I realized God had led me from California to Minnesota to receive training at an affordable, wonderful school where I would meet David and become his wife. Our vision to be missionaries was the same one, and God was confirming our future together.

God, my heavenly Father, had been guiding me all along by supernatural means. Out of my helplessness He came down, visited me and revealed the path ahead as I walked it.

I went home once in the summer to tell my parents about my engagement. Though Leonard was famous the world over, they had never heard of the Ravenhill family. They also were not comfortable that I was aligned with Holiness Pentecostal teaching. But I believed in—and had experienced—the baptism and gifts of the Holy Spirit, and my joy was not tarnished by their lack of enthusiasm.

They must have been curious, though, because they came to visit me at the school. As soon as they met the Ravenhill family they grew supportive.

A dear woman in her seventies told me that the Lord had directed her to buy material for my wedding dress. Another woman offered to make it. It was lovely: knee-length and made of silk brocade. I had a small hat with a white veil and white heels. I used some pink lipstick that day to brighten my face.

We were married at Bethany Missionary Church, and my parents paid for our reception, which was held in the school's dining room. It was a wonderful day for David and me.

I did not know on that happy day in August 1964 that I was to experience another dimension of the supernatural. God had promised that He would be with me all of my life. Three years later, I would meet Him in death.

6

ETERNITY!

For thus says the High and Lofty One who inhabits Eternity, whose name is Holy; I dwell in the high and holy place, with him who has a contrite and humble spirit, to revive the spirit of the humble, and to revive the heart of the contrite ones.

Isaiah 57:15 NKJV

Now, therefore, you are no more strangers and foreigners, but fellow citizens with the saints and members of the household of God

Ephesians 2:19 NKJV

Mrs. Ravenhill? This way."

I rose with difficulty from my chair in the hospital lobby, and with a quick look back at David and my mother, followed the nurse down a long hall toward maternity quarters for those who could not pay for hospital services.

In spite of our financial lack, I had never been happier. David and I had met David and Gwen Wilkerson shortly before we were married and heard the Lord calling us to join their Teen Challenge ministry in New York City.

David Wilkerson and Leonard Ravenhill were both speakers at a Full Gospel Business Men's conference in Denver, and had become instant friends. Leonard had brought back an early copy of *The Cross and the Switchblade*, and we were captivated by the story of the ministry, begun just five years earlier on the streets of New York for drug addicts, prostitutes and gang members like Nicky Cruz.

So in September, right after our honeymoon, David and I packed our few things and drove across the country in the big Chevy that his parents had given us as a wedding present.

The first weekend in Brooklyn, we took Nicky to a meeting in Pennsylvania where he spoke. We returned to our apartment to find that our wedding presents had been stolen. Nothing could be replaced, so we were starting out with little but our willingness to serve.

A few months later, Leonard and Martha also heard the Lord's call to work with Teen Challenge and so, after seven years at Bethany Fellowship, they followed us to New York.

I sought out my father-in-law in his office one day. He gave me a quick hug and a warm smile and then motioned me to a chair. As we chatted, I began to tell him how I had led a sheltered life and felt inadequate—even afraid—to work with people in such desperate need.

Leaning forward and speaking in his beautiful British accent with his usual conviction, he said these words: "Nancy, remember: A man or a woman with an experience is never at the mercy of a man or a woman with an argument." Then we discussed what he had just told me. His wise counsel and fervent teaching for the Church to be bold in her mission helped me get through my life in New York, as well as the years ahead. Over the years, David and I quoted these words to each other, especially in the difficult times of our lives.

David Wilkerson showed great love for the Ravenhills, and welcomed us all.

Leonard, who continued his traveling ministry as the Lord directed, also created and edited *Teen Challenge* magazine. Leonard wrote and compiled the articles, and David did everything else as far as layout and production, handing the finished magazine off to other departments for distribution.

Leonard and Martha's oldest son, Paul, and his wife, Irene, joined the staff to translate materials into Spanish. Phil, the youngest Ravenhill son, though still in high school, traveled around to various churches to show a movie about the work of Teen Challenge to build support.

I worked in the office. I had had no training for this, but I could type really well. Office work at that time was not that high tech.

Each of us at Teen Challenge had a part to play in the difficult, but amazing ministry to help drug addicts and prostitutes out of their pain and misery. They came in desperation to the Teen Challenge Center on Clinton Avenue in Brooklyn where, by God's grace, we saw them surrender their drugs, get their lives cleaned up, be filled with the Holy Spirit and then begin to follow Jesus Christ.

Three nights a week, David and I drove the ministry van filled with Teen Challenge workers to Catacomb Chapel in Greenwich Village where we ministered for at least three hours, getting home around midnight. People would come in for free coffee and sit at little tables. The only requirement for "patrons" was that conversations be around the subject of knowing Christ. David also worked on other days during the week at his prison ministry on Riker's Island.

When, after about eighteen months, we learned that our family was going to expand, we were very excited. I phoned my parents to tell them the good news about the upcoming arrival of the new baby, and my mother made plans right away to come and visit me. My father did not come to the phone, but Mother said that he was happy.

Several months before my due date, David and I took the subway to Glad Tidings Church, an Assemblies of God church in Manhattan. We used to visit different churches in the city on Sunday nights—the churches were alive with the presence of the Lord—and this spring evening we made our way to seats near the front. The speaker was a man named Loren Cunningham, who was going to talk about a new ministry he had recently begun called Youth With A Mission. His office was the back seat of his car!

As Loren talked about putting a team together, I heard the Lord speak to me: *You need to talk with him. I want you to work with him.*

I nudged David. He leaned in close, and I whispered what the Lord had told me.

He nodded. This was not a complete surprise to us. For a few months we had known that our time at Teen Challenge was drawing to a close. We were looking for direction, and hoped that our next venture might lead us to the South Pacific.

Personally, I had never considered going to the South Pacific—other than imagining the lives of the children in the big blue book about the silver bird—but it was David's dream, and as I was married to him now it became our dream together.

When the Sunday night service ended, David and I made our way to the back of the church where Loren was greeting people. We introduced ourselves, explaining that we felt the Lord might be directing us to offer ourselves to help with his ministry.

As we talked with him that night, we learned that the South Pacific was on Loren's heart as well! We felt sure that we had the Lord's leading.

Later that week, Loren visited us at Teen Challenge and then we met him at Bethany Fellowship that same month. We introduced him to staff there and talked happily about the future. Our child was due to be born in about a month. As soon after that as we could travel, we would go to New Zealand and become involved with this new ministry.

My mother had arrived in June for the birth of our baby and was living with us in our apartment in Brooklyn. It was wonderful to see that she had recovered her health. The dry desert air had been good for her.

I, on the other hand, was living in exhaustion. I attributed this to the unending work within a street drug culture where death toyed cruelly with its victims. I worked past my due date, but still the baby did not come. I was not too worried; I knew very little about giving birth. But I got larger and larger. I had gained only fifteen pounds, but I was very swollen.

Finally, early one morning, the time came. Since we worked for a nonprofit organization and our bank account held only a few hundred dollars, we could think of no other solution for us than a particular hospital that accepted patients who could not pay.

David and I drove in the dark with my mother, arriving at the hospital a little before 5:30 in the morning. As we parted, David and my mother went into the waiting room, and I struggled to keep up with the unsmiling nurse who led the way into a room to be prepped.

She handed me paper slippers and a gown and, as I labored to change, called periodically through the door, "Get done in there. I'm waiting here for you and don't have all day."

Next I was guided to a hallway of little rooms for women having contractions. The nurse told me that I could scream in there—and, indeed, as we walked past the closed doors I heard other women on the verge of delivery screaming in pain. I had been warned about contractions in labor. As I eased myself onto the bed I tried not to scream, but I could not help moaning ceaselessly.

I was in agony. I knew the baby was coming very, very fast. It actually scared me as I not only felt terrific pain, but also could not help hearing the screams of the other women in the nearby rooms. When the doctor came in I tried to communicate with him, but realized he could not speak English very well. The nurses helped translate, and he indicated that the baby was coming too fast.

I said in desperation, tears spilling from my eyes, "Just put me out!"

The doctor inserted a huge needle into my arm, and I never knew another thing until after the birth, about two hours after my arrival at the hospital.

Waking slightly and barely able to raise myself up, I saw that I was in a bed near the entrance of a large ward, just inside two big swinging doors. I wondered where my baby was, and why I was alone. I also wondered if I had given birth to a girl or boy.

I found out later that David had been informed that the delivery was completed, so he had taken my mother back to Teen Challenge. They knew that we had an eight-pound, two-ounce little girl, and that I was now resting in the ward. They planned to get a quick nap and return to the hospital that afternoon.

I opened my eyes wider to focus on a row of tall windows at the far end of the ward. Silhouetted against the early morning sunlight were two dozen or so iron beds with chipped green paint; patients were in all of them. I looked at the pained faces and felt compassion for these women.

A nurse came and took my pulse several times. It did not occur to me to tell her that I had the sense of fading away, and that I was extremely weak.

When she came the next time, I heard her stricken voice calling for emergency personnel. The hospital sounds grew more and more distant, and I grew less and less concerned about my life on this earth.

Quietly and quickly I left my body. I slipped out right through the top of my head. This did not seem at all unusual. I began traveling up through a narrow tunnel.

The tunnel felt like a confined place—maybe four feet across—that went up at an angle. When I say *up*, I mean within the spiritual realm. It felt as if my "self"—my soul and spirit—were vertically straight. I was traveling headfirst, my arms at my side.

On either side of me was an angel. I heard the sounds—the fluttering and flapping of their wings. I did not look at the angels; nor did I realize that I had died and left my body. I knew only that I was traveling somewhere. It was like night, but I could see clearly as we moved through the tunnel and up to eternity.

It did not take long to get where we were going. Here I was suspended in weightlessness. The area was massive and seemed to be outdoors. I wondered where I was. The thought crossed my mind that it was unusual to be there and not back in the green iron bed in the ward.

My interest grew in this unusual place. I was clothed—my spiritual body was covered. Rather than look with my eyes, I asked the Lord, *What am I wearing?*

I heard the Lord's voice answer me: *I've put you in your favorite dress.* I knew, simultaneously with His speaking, that I was wearing my white and blue striped sheath.

Even though I stood there calmly observing eternity, I still did not realize that I had died. Time did not exist. Time did not matter anymore. It was gone. There was great peace.

Still floating, I turned to look over my right shoulder. There ahead in a beautiful bright place at the edge of the holy city, quite a distance away, I saw perhaps thirty people. They were literally jumping up and down on the ground and waving at me. They seemed to have light within themselves.

I said to myself, *How do they know I am here?*

I heard no answer this time, but they clearly knew me and were expecting me.

My intelligence was more acute in this place; I knew a lot more. I knew, for instance, that they were in heaven and that I was in some outer place like a waiting room. My eyesight was also stronger; their joyful faces were clearly in view. They waved excitedly as though thrilled to see me.

From the crowd, a small woman with a hat on her head who looked to be about thirty years old moved in my direction. After a sound, like the clang of a gate, she floated lightly over toward me. I knew, without having to think, that she was my German grandmother—my father's mother, Agusta Schultz—whom I had never met; she had died before I was born. My father was her only child born in America.

I was completely enthralled! She kept pumping her arms and hands up and down trying to tell me that she loved me and wanted to hug me. Then she indicated that there was an invisible wall between us. They were on the edge of heaven and could not come where I was. I had the sense that this was not an area they visited often.

It was exciting to see her because I had heard so much about her and her prayer life as well as her service to God.

She glided back after telling me again with her smiling face and open arms that she loved me and wanted to hug me, but was not able to touch me. The Lord took her back and the gate clanged again. He must have put her in proximity to me for those few moments just so she could see me.

It was a wonderful scene before me. They looked like relatives from way back, people from the generations behind me, and seemed to be having some kind of a party. They wore modern-day clothes and were standing in rows waving and smiling.

Their thoughts entered my mind. Over and over they said, *We're so thrilled you are here! We can't wait to see you and meet you!* If this was the cloud of witnesses that the Bible speaks of, then it felt like my "own" cloud. They were observing me and had a connection to me. The personal connection felt real—and divine. The Lord is so personal!

Then my grandmother left, going back to join the others in the beautiful place of heaven. I still hung suspended in this dark waiting place, floating like an astronaut in outer space.

I am not sure where my next words came from. Anything my mind thought became actions. I thought, *Turn*, and I turned.

There was Jesus. He was watching me. He was smiling. His expression showed such sweetness.

The angels who had escorted me were with Him. They looked like women with beautiful faces. One of them was standing beside Him, speaking secrets into His ear. His head was bent slightly toward her as she talked to Him, but He kept His eyes on me and seemed to be enjoying having me there.

The other angel stood back several feet behind the first angel and was praying. They exuded absolute humility. It flowed from them. Their graceful white wings, extending out from their long white clothes, were folded neatly behind them.

Jesus sat in a chair that was thick and wide and looked solid. It was like a throne, but it was not carved or ornate; I sensed that it was pure gold. He looked relaxed.

He was wearing a long white robe, which was lit up. That is to say, He was light. He did not look like a movie star—the way He is portrayed on film. Rather, as Scripture says, His visage is lowly. Isaiah 53:2 tells us that when He walked on earth "there was nothing beautiful or majestic about his appearance, nothing to attract us to him" (NLT). At the same time, though, His face was beautiful to me. We will love the way He looks.

As soon as I saw Him, I began talking to Him. This was no different from the many times I had talked with Him on earth. I spoke eagerly and with conviction. "Jesus," I said, "I've just had a baby and I need at least eighteen years to raise this child. I want to go back to earth." My heart was also saying, *I'll come later, if You want me.* For a long time I wondered if He would call me back home after the eighteen years had passed, but that was not the case.

Even though it was so peaceful and lovely there, I wanted to go back to earth. And I think that I was meant to go back down; my work on earth was not completed. Actually, He must have prepared me not to want to stay.

Before I could think another syllable, the Lord had turned me 180 degrees and I was traveling back down to earth. I was once again moving quickly in a narrow space—feet first this time! I heard the angels' wings on either side of me.

Back in the ward, I reentered my body just as I had left— through the top of my head. I filled my body once again. My eyelids opened and I was able to focus. The scene looked to me like the shutter shots of the early days of film—the fluttering light and dark of consciousness and unconsciousness.

Doctors and nurses surrounded my bed. A few had their masks covering their faces. They all seemed to exhale with relief and someone shouted, "Get her back to the operating room!"

At this, I felt them literally lift my bed and lunge through the double doors. I fell into unconsciousness and did not wake up again until two days later.

When I opened my eyes at last, it was wonderful to see my mother and my mother-in-law at my side. I was in a lab area, where I had been for those two days getting blood transfusions. They were both crying, and said together, "We almost lost you."

I asked what had happened and learned that toxicity had apparently overtaken my body. That explained the bloating.

They were not sure exactly why I had died, but had been told that I had suffered significant internal hemorrhaging. Our few hundred dollars were given toward the cost of the blood.

I was so weak I said little. A nurse asked if I would like to see my daughter—I was overjoyed to learn that we had a little girl!

Since I was now awake and out of danger, the nurses took me back to the ward. Visitors were not allowed, but they let David in to see me.

David and I had not picked out a name. We were so unprepared. It turned out that David and Leonard actually named her. By the time I got back into the ward all the forms were signed and gone. David had begun calling her Lisa, and Leonard favored the name Lynn. So Lisa Lynn Ravenhill was welcomed into our family.

My mother kept herself busy trying to locate blood donors for me. She went all over Teen Challenge, asking every addict she saw if he or she would donate blood. She never figured out that this was not the safest source of supply!

The nurse who had found me dead came to me one day. She leaned down and said quietly, "Where did you go?"

I could only shake my head. I did not know how to speak of it. For many years I never told anyone except David what had happened to me.

I thought about it though. Over and over I pondered the extraordinary experience. I recalled, too, my father-in-law's words when I had been afraid of serving in the difficult environment we faced in New York City: *A man or a woman with an experience is never at the mercy of a man or a woman with an argument.*

I knew that after this experience I could never be tempted to doubt the reality of heaven—regardless of any argument that might present itself. I can still picture in my mind's eye the sounds, the angels, the warm and happy smiles of those waiting with eager and welcoming hugs.

And Jesus.

Heaven felt so close. But our hearts were set on our new work half a world away.

7

BLESSING THE LITTLE ONES

Then they also brought infants to Him that He might touch them; but when the disciples saw it, they rebuked them. But Jesus called them to Him and said, "Let the little children come to Me, and do not forbid them; for of such is the kingdom of God. Assuredly, I say to you, whoever does not receive the kingdom of God as a little child will by no means enter it."

Luke 18:15–17 NKJV

"See that you do not despise one of these little ones, for I say to you that their angels in heaven continually see the face of My Father who is in heaven."

Matthew 18:10

When I left the hospital and arrived back at Teen Challenge, some of the newer people who had seen me so bloated during the pregnancy barely recognized me. I was still recovering, still sore and could not walk well. "Is that really you?" they said. I heard this more than once!

One night when Lisa was about a month old, the doorbell of our apartment rang, and David went to answer it.

There stood my father.

I was shocked. He had not let us know he was coming even though we had spoken by phone a few times over the previous weeks. He was en route to Norway—one of his nearly dozen evangelistic trips there.

We invited him to stay the night, and I wondered how we could commune in peace even that long. Little Lisa was a helpful point of contact for us; he seemed genuinely to adore her. He asked questions about our apartment and talked excitedly with Leonard, inviting him on trips like this one to Norway.

After Daddy left, David and I marveled at this time together without tempests. Mother had told me that he had mellowed, and I was happy to believe that it might be so.

Lisa was growing every day. It took more weeks for me to regain my strength, but soon, with the blessing and help of our friends at Teen Challenge, David and I began packing our suitcases and the three barrels of belongings that would be shipped separately.

At last, on a warm fall day, we were ready. Lisa was only three months old when the three of us boarded a freighter in New York Harbor that would take us halfway around the world. Twelve passengers were allowed on the ship; most of us were emigrating from the United States to go live in New Zealand and Australia.

It was a miracle that we were able to book passage. We were told that we would not be allowed to travel with a baby unless there was a doctor on board. Two weeks before we were hoping to leave, a couple from Christchurch, New Zealand, a doctor and his wife, booked the last two slots and graciously fulfilled our medical requirement.

We said a tearful good-bye to David's parents, and made the way to our quarters—a beautiful stateroom with an attached bathroom. It was very luxurious to us. Lisa's fold-up canvas bed was placed at the foot of our bed.

For more than a month the freighter steamed down the East Coast of America and then journeyed westward through the Panama Canal toward New Zealand. For almost half of the trip, we saw no land. Finally we arrived—at the bottom of the earth.

Our friends Gayle and Geoff Stevens met us at the dock in Auckland and drove us to Hamilton, a beautiful city on the mainland. Gayle's aunt and uncle had a home there and invited us to live with them in preparation for our move to the Barrier Island, which was about fifty miles off the northeast shore of New Zealand and the place where our work would begin.

During the six weeks that we lived in Hamilton, the house seemed to stretch and bend for all our needs. Gayle's aunt and uncle, who lived upstairs—as did Gayle and Geoff with their little boy—were very kind to us. They provided a room in their basement that had a crib for Lisa, a table where we ate our meals and a couch in the corner that folded down to make a bed at night. It was cozy and warm and the room had windows that brought in lots of light from the early summer days.

Gayle's parents owned land on the Barrier Island, where they had set up a ministry center for people with spiritual and physical needs. They graciously offered this as a base for us to use while we worked to establish the YWAM head-quarters for the South Pacific. Gayle and Geoff went to the island first to work on the house we two families would be sharing. David and I would follow in a couple of weeks, a few days before Christmas.

Our first job, though, having newly arrived in Hamilton, was getting Lisa acclimated. I was unable to breastfeed, and that meant she needed to drink powdered milk.

The problem was the milk. No matter how much we stirred or mashed it in water, it simply would not get smooth; lumps seemed to form and harden in her bottle.

Lisa was a healthy baby and quite hungry. When I gave her the powdered milk, she would gulp it down even if it meant swallowing lumps. I worried about her at first, but she did not seem to have any trouble and slept peacefully. I was grateful, since there was really no alternative if we were to live and work on the island.

While Lisa seemed to be doing well, the acclimation was exhausting for David and me. Everything was different. We were not only going into conditions that we had never experienced but also initiating a new work.

One night, with Lisa sleeping soundly in her crib, so sweet and snug in her little pink jumpsuit, David and I put the sheets and blanket on the couch and fell into bed. We were asleep almost instantly.

Around midnight I sensed someone standing near me by the side of the bed. There was no light in the room, and I assumed it was David tending to something. I turned over and fell again into deep sleep.

A hand on my shoulder, shaking me roughly, brought me to consciousness. I lifted my head and could distinguish in the darkness that the form jumped back and away from me so that I could get out of the bed.

I knew that something was urgent and was alert instantly. I thought that David was pressing me to get up quickly. "Oh, what's wrong?" I said, throwing back the covers. I hurried to the wall and turned on the overhead light to check on Lisa.

She was lying on her tummy. I could not imagine how she had turned over, but then I saw with horror that she was face-down in a big puddle of powdered milk.

"David, look!" I said, quickly lifting her. "Lisa has thrown up her milk!" Near panic, I checked her breathing. She coughed a little, and made little choking noises, but then began breathing normally.

"She must have rolled over," I said, feeling myself shaking. I held her and studied her little body intently. "Her face was in all that liquid. She could have smothered!" I kept chattering to David nervously as I found a towel and began to clean her and her bedding.

"I'll wash all this tomorrow," I said, putting her soiled clothing and bedding aside. I dressed her in clean nightclothes and laid her down carefully. She fell sound asleep. "Well, we might as well go back to bed."

It was only then that I turned and saw that David had never stirred. In all that commotion, he had slept unmoving with his back toward me.

Then I realized that someone else was in the room, someone I could not see. I stood frozen, aware of a messenger from heaven. I had chills up and down my spine. I was too afraid even to get back into bed.

I waited. I did not see this angel, but felt his protective presence. I knew that he was watching me. Finally, I walked slowly to the light switch, clicked the room back into darkness and crawled under the covers.

When I told David the next morning, our hearts were grateful at this powerful indication of the Lord's presence with us. We had to continue to give Lisa the powdered milk—squashing the lumps on the side of a bowl with a wooden spoon—but never had another incident with it.

The simple wooden house that we were going to share with Gayle and Geoff was shipped over to the mainland on a flat barge. It was floated into the Bay on big metal drums and deposited near the shoreline. It was quite an old house. Part of the roof of the house was open, but our bedrooms were enclosed.

Once the house was in place, David, Lisa and I crossed the rough waters of the Hauraki Gulf to begin life on the Island. To work at the main house or meet with the others for lunch and dinner, we had to traverse rocks and a small hill. Or, if the tide was out, we could just run along the beach.

David hung a massive clothesline. We dragged our dirty clothes in baskets to the main house for washing (the washing machine was run by a generator), and then dragged them back to hang them on the line. I washed Lisa's diapers in the Pacific Ocean every day. The wind was amazing. I always wondered how the clothes stayed on the line.

There was no electricity, so we used Tilley lamps at night. We had a wood-burning stove to heat the house; it took David hours of cutting wood to get the stove hot enough to bake a cake.

The work was exhilarating, but after fourteen months, while fasting and praying, we sensed that it was God's timing for us to return to the States. A home in Ponsonby would serve as the new Youth With A Mission base for the next year. We had accomplished our goal of seeing that YWAM was set up in the South Pacific, and now we would be heading to Anaheim, California, to work with YWAM there.

Thus, the three of us flew back to the States and settled into an apartment in Buena Park, California. David worked in the YWAM office, running a printing press. I continued to do typing either at home or at the office in Anaheim. I brought Lisa to work with me, and she played with her toys around my desk. It was great to have real milk again.

My parents were about one hundred miles away and came down occasionally from the Mojave Desert to see us. Our times together were tenuous. My mother looked frail, but loved seeing the three of us. She and my father doted on Lisa, but he still found it difficult to communicate with me in a loving way.

I could never figure out why he would get so angry. He never seemed to get over his problem with me. Mother would tell me how he was changing, and I was glad to hear that he was feeling fulfilled in his ministry in Norway. Ultimately, God helped me navigate the pain that flooded me when I was with him; I seemed always on the verge of being swept away by his rejection. When I felt afraid, I knew that Jesus would see me through, as He had promised.

David's parents also came from their home in Illinois to visit us occasionally and stay with us in our tiny apartment. They helped in any way they could. Martha was a wonderful cook and loved to bake. She also was a big help with all the washing and ironing. She never stopped working! Leonard spent much time in prayer, writing or preparing to speak.

Before long, we had the happy news that another baby was on the way.

Because I had died and come back to life three years earlier when Lisa was born, and because we now had some income, we made a search and found a wonderfully kind and experienced doctor.

As our second little girl came to birth, and I watched the amazing delivery by way of a mirror, the doctor laughed out loud and said to me, "Look at that!" She was coming into this world crying and screaming at the top of her lungs as she breathed her first whiff of air. She looked healthy and normal, and that was all I cared about as her mother. She was a beautiful baby.

Soon I was taken back to my big hospital room (the room had four beds, but I had it to myself), and David arrived with Lisa in his arms. My parents followed behind him. They were thrilled about having another little granddaughter. They all stood around my bed smiling, and as I looked up at my mother I said on impulse, "Mother, would you like to name this baby? If David and I like the name, we'll use it."

My mother's face lit up. I could see her eyes soften as she said, "Oh, I've thought the name Christine Elizabeth would be so beautiful for your little girl."

Then I said as I looked at David, "I like that name, but would like it spelled with a *K*."

David said, "Well, I've wanted the name to be Tina for months. We could name her Kristine, but let's call her Tina."

My father did not speak, but he was smiling. It felt like a moment of healing for our family.

When everyone left for the evening, I got out of bed and walked over to the window, waving at them as they got into their cars. David was still holding Lisa. They both looked up at me in the window and waved. How I wanted to go with them! But I had to stay in the hospital at least one night.

I crawled back into bed and lay quietly thinking. Tina was in a tiny crib at my side. I was very happy that Lisa would go through life with a little sister. And I was glad for the peace I felt toward my parents.

Movement in the corner of the room caught my eye.

I saw Jesus.

He stood in His long white robe. I locked my eyes onto Him, looking intently at Him, amazed. He then spoke to me about the new baby. I heard Him give me a promise about Tina's future, and I listened with all my heart.

He did not just state the promise one time; He repeated it over and over. I could imagine He said it at least fifty times. I knew that He did not want me to forget it. I loved hearing His voice, so I just lay still, listening to the sentence He kept giving me.

After a few minutes I watched Him walk past the end of my bed and right out the door. The moment He left the room, I turned my head and fell into a deep sleep.

I learned through this experience—by His many repetitions of the promise—to continue to remind the Lord of His words over and over again until they come true in my life. Every promise in His Word is true; He is the faithful God. This helps us trust Him for the future when we cannot see Him at work.

People often ask me why Jesus appears to me. They wonder if He will appear to them, too. I have no good answer for either question. As I have learned the hard way, God is God. He can do anything He wants! But I do know that He wants us to believe that He is always with us, whether we see Him or not.

When I ask myself why Jesus appeared to me that first time when I was five years old, I think of a verse from Matthew 5, when Jesus taught His disciples that the pure in heart are blessed. On that day, the first of many terrible whippings from my father, I turned to Jesus and affirmed who He was, praising Him without even realizing it. I think that God saw purity in a little five-year-old who was turning to Him in her pain.

But remember, seeing Him does not mean that our problems simply melt away. Sometimes God delivers us out of our troubles, but sometimes He allows the situation to get worse and worse. The brutal whippings from my father did not stop simply because I came to Jesus. My childhood did not change. In fact, there were times I doubted I would survive. My father studied the Word and wanted to teach it, but he did not apply it to himself. He did not take responsibility for His family.

Seeing how my father missed many blessings because of his poor decisions helped me understand that we need to keep our lives pure before God—like little children. Do we believe Scripture? Do we live out our confession? God is the High Priest of our confession. He wants us to live as though we believe that to be true—regardless of the circumstances.

Do you find this easier said than done? I know I do. After God rescued Lisa from suffocating in the powdered milk, for instance, or after Tina was born and I heard the wonderful promise that He wanted me to pray to fulfillment, I wondered many times why I never told anyone about the supernatural experiences. I think David's parents (surely) and my parents (probably) would have been touched and encouraged by that.

But my fear of being rejected or dismissed won out. And it militated against something good that God might have wanted me to do. I held back when I could have been a blessing to our family, sharing about God's goodness and mercy.

Fear has had the final word too many times in my life. I learned from my early years just to be quiet. I never wanted to ruffle any feathers or say something out of the ordinary. As you will see in the chapters that follow, there were more encounters with Jesus and His angelic host, more experiences of guidance, healing, encouragement that by telling might have brought hope to others. But in my fear I kept quiet.

I have learned, though, that when I blow it I can run to the Lord Jesus and my heart will be set free. Staying focused on Christ Jesus with childlike faith helps us keep our lives pure before Him.

God forgives our iniquities every single day. I love Psalm 103 with its words of promise that God loads our lives with His "benefits": "Bless the LORD, O my soul . . . who forgives all your iniquities, who heals all your diseases, who redeems your life from destruction, who crowns you with lovingkindness and tender mercies" (verses 2–4 NKJV).

If we believe in the saving work of His shed blood, we will more easily believe that His love is operating in our lives.

Jesus' name is all-powerful. And look at this marvel: He has "magnified [His] word above all [His] name" (Psalm 138:2 NKJV). The New Living Translation says that His "promises are backed by all the honor of [His] name." This means that Jesus has given us everything we need to live lives of purity:

The name saves.

The blood cleanses.

The Word strengthens.

This helped me trust Jesus completely, knowing that what He told me He will do. Deuteronomy 7:9 says: "Know therefore that the LORD your God, He is God, the faithful God who keeps His covenant and His lovingkindness to a thousandth generation with those who love Him and keep His commandments."

When we glorify God, He comes right down into our midst. Scripture says that God is enthroned upon the praises of His people (see Psalm 22:3). "Whoever offers praise glorifies Me; and to him who orders his conduct aright I will show the salvation of God" (Psalm 50:23 NKJV).

Even if we cannot see Him, He is there. And when we call on His name, believe in His blood and keep His Word alive in our hearts, He will help us be pure like little children. Not perfect, but pure.

8

A STRANGER IN THE NIGHT

Last night an angel of the God to whom I belong . . . stood beside me.

Acts 27:23 NLT

It was time to move again.

We began to prepare for missionary work in New Guinea at the YWAM base in Port Moresby. Lisa was now four years old, and Tina almost two. They kept us busy, but miraculously on this particular evening they had both settled down and were sleeping quietly.

The little white stucco house we rented was not far from the Southern California mountains in a town called La Crescenta. We had almost no money but the rent was reasonable. It was a humble little house with a large garage and workshop in the big backyard, which was also full of apricot trees. There were even swings for Lisa to play on.

The only odd thing was the decision our next-door neighbor made to begin construction of his new house alongside the huge pine trees that lined our driveway, which in turn bordered our house. I say that it was odd, because there was plenty of room to place the house more centrally on his land. The construction looked to be about halfway completed. The outside framing was covered with insulation, and holes were cut into the walls where windows and doors would go.

Frankly, though, we gave his construction project little thought. It was 1971, and things were beautiful in that time on the earth in Southern California. More peaceful. I remember taking my father-in-law down to Montrose to show him around—especially to point out all the banks. There were banks everywhere. I talked about the little bit of money I had placed in one of these impressive establishments, and he laughed with me. But I was always trying to be cautious and save for the future.

We had now lived in California for about three and a half years. I was proud of David's work with YWAM. Anything they needed him to do, he could do. He was artistic and gifted at writing, printing, binding. Summers he would travel and be gone for weeks at a time, knocking on doors to share the Good News. He was very shy, but he knew the call of God on his life.

Though it was pleasant to have a house with electricity and indoor plumbing after life on the Barrier Island, we still looked forward to returning to the mission field. For the moment, though, we welcomed sleep, glad for the long and, we hoped, quiet night ahead.

At midnight we both awoke with a start. Sirens blared as fire trucks rumbled down our street and stopped near our house. We pulled back the curtains over our bedroom window and watched wide-eyed as firemen attached a hose to the hydrant on our street and moved inside the big empty house next door.

After some minutes, the firemen came back out and began checking the yard and perimeter of the property. They had apparently caught the problem early, perhaps thanks to some alert neighbor. Their big trucks, with the bright rotating lights still flashing, drove away.

Not a peep had come from the girls through all this, so we pulled the curtains shut, settled back gratefully once more and went to sleep.

At four o'clock I woke again. This time I heard no noise outside, nothing discernible that might have awakened me, but I had the oddest thought: *If this is an angel, I want to get a good look at him.* How utterly peculiar! Instantly, there was a loud banging at the front door.

David was awake now, too, and we grabbed our robes and hurried to the living room. David opened the front door, and there stood a man nicely dressed in slacks and an open-collared shirt. He was wearing street shoes, and to our perplexed look offered his explanation.

"That's my van over there," he said quickly, pointing to a vehicle a good block from our house. "I was just driving by because I'm on my way to go fishing." I barely had time to think but noticed that he hardly looked like someone going fishing. He continued quickly, pointing to the neighboring house. "Look, you've got to get out. The house next door is on fire!"

Even as he spoke, we saw—and heard—it. Flames raged through the empty house, leaping out from windows and doors and up through the roof. Everything seemed to be popping, snapping, melting in a great roar. What was more, the fire was spreading to the top of the pine trees between us. Our house was no more than the width of our driveway from the roaring flames.

We knew this man would help us even though we did not take the time to exchange words. David and I flew to the girls' bedroom. David picked up Lisa, and I picked up little Tina. David needed to call the fire department, so he put Lisa into the stranger's arms and hurried to the phone. The stranger and I, taking the children, went out the door, through the front yard and across the street, where we stood and watched the incredible scene before us.

I could not think about anything except that the house was going to burn down. I was so flummoxed I began talking nervously. I had never seen anything like this except in a movie. The man said nothing in response. But then I looked up at the sky and saw, as if in a vision, these words written in large red letters: *Your house will be saved.*

I wish I could say that I was bolstered by faith at this odd occurrence, but I had nothing but fear in my heart as plumes of fire and smoke lit the night sky around us with a surreal glow. Lisa snuggled quietly in the man's arms, watching wide-eyed. Tina was quiet in my arms.

After David emerged from our house, he began to knock on neighbors' doors to let them know the danger and also to see if there was anyone who might help. We really had no idea what to do. The fire department had not arrived. He got the hose and started trying to soak our roof with water.

The tops of the trees along the driveway were snapping and crackling in the blaze.

At this the man spoke: "What is your husband doing?"

"He's getting help . . . the trees . . ."

"Oh, no."

"But the house . . ." I said again with a helpless gesture.

At that moment a police car came within sight. The officer stopped instantly and radioed the fire department. Within barely a minute the fire trucks roared onto our street once more and began blasting water on the burning house and trees. By this time about fifty neighbors, most in robes and slippers, stood on the street, asking questions, wondering what had happened, offering help.

The fire was at last put out. It never made the short hop from the trees to our house. God had spared us.

David came up to us and said to the stranger, "Can I take my little girl now?" David extended his arms and, with the barest hesitation, the stranger leaned forward and placed Lisa gently into them.

By this time, the welcome edge of morning on the horizon dispelled some of my fears. A neighbor motioned to me to come and talk with her, but I was reluctant to leave this stranger who had helped us so immensely. I then remembered my odd thought upon awakening: *If this is an angel, I want to get a good look at him.* I turned and stared at him, unabashedly, for about thirty seconds. He stared back, calmly, not saying a word.

My neighbor was calling me over and I felt I should go to her. I turned in her direction just as David was turning to the stranger, intending to thank him. But the man was not there. He had simply disappeared. We looked down the street; the van was also gone.

Several neighbors standing nearby posed the question on our own minds: "Where did he go?" We could only shake our heads in amazement.

Finally, with the light of morning filling the sky, the fire department told us that it was safe to return home. David and I sat on the turquoise living room rug with Lisa and Tina and started to worship God, thanking Him for protecting us. We lifted our voices and our hands, so grateful for what He had done. We knew that He had sent an angel to save us from disaster.

Later in the day, I was walking around the house with the girls when I saw new cause for rejoicing. Around our bedroom window, the one on the side of the house by the fire, was something like a halo, a yellow scorch mark about an inch wide in the otherwise unsinged stucco. It looked as if it had been drawn on with a yellow marker except that it had the look of fire in it.

It was awesome to me. I knew it was a sign that the Lord had come the night before, visiting us and leaving the mark of His divine protection. Standing there with our little girls, I was nearly brought to tears with gratitude. I wanted to take a picture, but my camera was already packed in a barrel ready for our departure to New Guinea.

The evening paper carried the story of the fire. It was indeed arson, our neighbor setting fire to his own house—twice! When the first attempt had failed, he had set another.

I cut out the story to send to David's parents, and when Leonard and Martha got my letter, they phoned us right away. We then learned more about God's amazing provision for our safety.

Leonard and Martha were staying in the house of a friend who lived in the Bahamas. The night of the fire, at midnight, they were awakened by three distinct knocks on their locked bedroom door. Leonard got up, pulled his trousers on and opened the door, but saw nothing. An experienced intercessor, he sensed a warning and began praying for his three sons' families who were living in various parts of the world. He prayed that God would intervene to protect us all from danger. After a while he went back to bed.

At four a.m., the same thing happened. Three loud knocks awakened them. Again Leonard got up, pulled on his trousers and opened the door. Again no one was there. He prayed fervently until he felt peace that God had acted to protect his children and grandchildren.

The story of the fire was all over town. People we had never met came to our door to talk about it. Our neighbors who had seen the stranger wondered about his presence—and disappearance. They knew something unusual had happened.

Even as we made the final preparations for the new life ahead of us, we talked of little else. We did not know that we were about to have another lesson in the supernatural—this time, the power of healing prayer.

9

THE GOD WHO HEALS

Thy children [shall be] like olive plants all around your table.

Psalm 128:3 NKJV

Give ear, O LORD, to my prayer; and attend to the voice of my supplications. In the day of my trouble I will call upon You, for You will answer me.

Psalm 86:6–7 NKJV

One of the few pictures taken of David and me on our wedding day shows us in front of the large map of the world hanging in the entryway of Bethany Missionary Church. There in our wedding finery, we are pointing to New Guinea, the large island in the South Pacific leapfrogging Australia.

David longed to minister there. I loved how he would laugh and say that he could not tell if the call came from God or

National Geographic. We had been quite close when we were in New Zealand, but now our prayer was literally coming true.

A couple of months after the fire, David and I had once more given away everything we owned, except for the contents of three barrels and a few suitcases for us and the girls. Lisa was now almost five, and Tina was two and a half. We boarded a plane in Los Angeles and settled in for the long legs of the flight. The children mostly slept as we flew. I looked out the window, watching nothing but water for hours. After landing in Brisbane, Australia, we boarded another plane that would take us to the capital city of Port Moresby, New Guinea. It was very warm that day.

And the light! It was the brightest sunlight I had ever seen. It seemed to "wake me up." It felt as though the Lord was nudging me to be alert, to be aware of where He was taking us. I felt the enormity of the privilege of serving God in this exotic land.

New Guinea, we knew, was a fascinating country of around four million people with more than seven hundred distinct languages, but I was not prepared for life there. It was a shock. On the one hand, the tropical beauty could take your breath away. Palm trees, lush grasses, blue sky. On the other hand, many people lived in unimaginable poverty and filth. We also heard regularly of tribes being discovered that had never seen anybody from the outside world.

The YWAM base of operations, which YWAM was purchasing, was a large house with a tiny apartment at ground level in a poor area of Port Moresby. Although the base was under good leadership, it was facing many difficulties in this land of so many poor and uneducated people. Our job was to help out in teaching, Bible study with the team and prayer, as well as do evangelistic work in the city and outlying areas. We eventually started a church that functioned from the base—the first church YWAM had ever begun.

We had little money—only $150.00 monthly coming in from Bethany Fellowship. That was the allotment for students who joined the church there and went onto the mission field. We loved the passion Bethany had to raise up missionaries.

Thus it was something of a miracle that, soon after we arrived, we were able to purchase our first home. It was across town and the cost was twelve thousand dollars. Our monthly mortgage was $150.00—exactly what we had guaranteed coming to us from Bethany. Somehow, mostly through gifts of money, we were able to buy a Jeep.

Our house stood on concrete pillars about ten feet off the ground. We had no air conditioning; it was like living in an oven. Being higher off the ground gave us a little better air circulation, as well as some protection from snakes.

After living there for about a year, we assumed leadership of the Youth With A Mission base, since the current leader was moving on to Japan.

When David took over, many thousands of dollars were due if the purchase of the base was to go through as planned. In the meantime, the government had allocated YWAM some nice land for a church building near the university. We decided to sell our house and give the money to the church building fund. That meant we could begin construction right away. Our family moved into the apartment under the base house at this time.

I have to admit that I was not looking forward to squeezing into such a tiny space. We were finally able to fit the girls' bunk beds into the kitchen.

But there were other challenges. Every night when David and I turned out the lights, about twenty large cockroaches would come out of hiding and scurry around our feet. We could only take off our flip-flops and whack them, killing them all before we could go to sleep.

The walls felt slimy in the steamy atmosphere and never got clean. When we took showers, we had to stand on a wooden slat to keep our feet out of the mucky water in the shower stall. The sewage from neighboring houses was a constant stench and bred a plethora of bugs, rats, mice. Thick green plants, called "the bush," grew everywhere. At times we had to hack our way through to make any sort of path.

Our greatest concern was the children. Even though they were inoculated and we did our best to keep everything clean, we could not always protect them from the diseases that swept through the area.

After about a year, the building of the church was coming along nicely, but slowly. Now only the roof needed to be constructed. We sensed at that point, with the base also in a stable position, that the Lord was leading us to go down to Christchurch, New Zealand, for an additional year of Bible school. As we made our plans, we considered the possibility of returning to continue helping with the work in New Guinea.

As we awaited the end of Lisa's school term—February in that part of the world—we booked passage on a ship that was coming through in a few weeks' time. We were all very skinny, but deeply tanned. Most of my clothes had disintegrated in the stifling heat. A kind woman gave me some beautiful new things to take with me.

So we began packing our barrels, choosing what to take, what to give away, zigzagging around the piles of clothes, pillows, sheets, vases, trinkets and our worn out shoes in the small living room. This was during the rainy season; the wind-driven sheets of water gave open invitation to the bugs, flies, rodents and cockroaches to seek shelter inside. The windows were closed against the rain, which added to the stifling heat and steam.

On one particular afternoon, just about a week before we were scheduled to leave, David took one of his last trips to pick up Lisa from school. I heard him return and come through the door, calling me.

He was helping Lisa inside. She did not look good. "What's wrong?" I asked.

David looked grim. "I don't know."

Lisa complained that her neck was sore and that she was very tired. A quick check indicated that she had a fever.

We helped her lie down on one of the bunk beds, and she soon fell asleep. Lying so still with her sweet face and blond hair down to her waist, she looked like a porcelain doll.

There was no extra room in our tiny kitchen, so David sat in a chair with Tina on his lap, and I climbed up onto the top bunk.

David and I began to pray. We had no idea what was wrong.

As we prayed, a word came to my mind: *meningitis*. I looked down at David. "I keep hearing the word *meningitis*. Do you know what it means?"

He shook his head. We wondered if this was even a normal word. All we knew for sure was that God had spoken to us and would help us understand.

Lisa awoke and her neck was stiffer. She was hardly able to move. We realized that we needed help.

The weather that evening was especially terrible. The torrential rain pounded the house; the palm trees and bush leaned this way and that as gusts of wind pushed and released the lush leaves.

David threw on his coat, ran out our door and around to the front door of the house to use the phone in our office. He returned shortly, hung up his dripping coat and told me that he had found a doctor's name in the phone book and reached him.

The doctor knew the address and had agreed to come immediately. We craned our necks looking out the window for him and felt some relief when he arrived. In just the time it took to get from his car at the front of the building down and around to our door, this wonderful Chinese doctor was soaked to the skin.

The doctor examined Lisa, and tried to help her sit up. She was not able to do so. After only a few minutes, he looked up at us. "Your daughter has meningitis," he said. "You must get her to the hospital immediately."

David and I exchanged glances. We had not mentioned this word to him. To us, this was a confirmation from God. He had spoken to us in answer to prayer. We knew to continue to pray and seek His help.

I found a blanket, which we wrapped around her for the trip.

"Find someone to take care of Tina," David said. "I'll come back for you." Shielding Lisa as best he could, David ran with her to the car. The doctor got into his car, and they drove away.

I got Tina settled and continued to call out to God, awaiting David's return. Before long I was riding with him in the Jeep, watching the windshield wipers swiping in vain against the pelting water.

The hospital had a thatched roof and few walls, but the children's ward was enclosed. As soon as I was with Lisa in her room, David returned to the base to set up a prayer meeting. At least twenty faithful YWAMers joined him to battle in prayer, weeping on their knees before the Lord.

The hours passed. Lisa fell asleep. I, too, continued to pray throughout the very long night. We knew now that she would not survive this terrible disease if God did not help us. I was certain that it was an attack, that the devil was sending fiery darts. I prayed for Lisa's immediate healing, for our future together as a family, for the YWAM base and everyone there. I knew we needed God's deliverance right then.

I turned around in my chair to look at a large black and white clock above my head. I stared glassy-eyed at the hands. It was five minutes to four in the morning.

At that moment a voice in my inner ear sliced through the silence. The Lord spoke to me. He said, *It's all over!*

I knew that something in the spirit world had broken. It had been a desperate battle, and God had answered our prayers. With a rejoicing heart, I then felt free to doze in my chair.

David joined us at the hospital a couple of hours later, and I relayed to him what I had heard God say.

The Chinese doctor arrived just before seven in the morning. Lisa was awake, and he began to examine her. Finally he looked at us and said confidently, "Mr. and Mrs. Ravenhill, whatever Lisa had wrong with her yesterday, it's gone. She does not have meningitis this morning." Then he said, "Give her something to eat."

I began to cry. I could not even speak. Lisa's energy was returning, and all she wanted to do was go home. The doctor released her, and we returned happily with Lisa back to the base. On this return trip, the clacking wipers sounded like happy beats of our hearts. For the next couple of days, she would wake up and eat something and then fall back asleep, but we knew she was regaining her strength.

It was truly a divine miracle. We saw firsthand that God can and does heal. We know absolutely that our Redeemer lives, and that He is the same yesterday, today and forever. We can testify that, "With God nothing shall be impossible" (Luke 1:37 KJV).

These verses and many others sustained us that night. They kept us from being consumed by fear and helped us believe that our God walks with us through hard times.

How then do we pray in times like this?

I believe that desperation is the key. David and I learned this years earlier as we began our work with Teen Challenge in New York City. Leonard would say, "God doesn't answer prayer; He answers desperate prayer." We had many opportunities to see that God hears a desperate heart. Excuses cannot get us to that position. God knows when we cannot make it without Him. Many times He meets us when we are at our wits' end and have exhausted all of our other resources.

In the situation with Lisa, I believe that the enemy was attacking because we knew we were in the Lord's will. We had a choice to make: Pray in faith for God to see us through or lose faith and be consumed.

Whenever we choose to forego sin and live by His Word, God will always guide us. He hears the sincere heart. But desperate prayer goes to another level. The person who is desperate and has to have an answer will get one. You know when you are on fire for God. It is the place where, if God does not answer this prayer, you cannot go through another day. Perhaps you, too, have been there.

In general—and this is true in my life far too often—I think that we are not desperate enough. We say our prayers—sometimes nonchalantly—every morning, but that is not being desperate.

This is why the supernatural is important to me. God is the only One who has the answers.

Andrew Murray made a wonderful observation. He said that when people pray, it is a sacrifice to God. Prayer is hard work. It is just as much of a sacrifice as witnessing or giving or preaching or teaching.

That is what is so unique about the Christian life: We walk by faith not by sight. Look at these promises from Scripture: "Let us hold fast the confession of our hope without wavering, for He who promised is faithful" (Hebrews 10:23 NKJV); "What He [has] promised He [is] also able to perform" (Romans 4:21 NKJV); "You, O Lord, are a God full of compassion, and gracious, longsuffering and abundant in mercy and truth" (Psalm 86:15 NKJV).

This does not mean that our prayers are always answered the way we want them to be. No, that is not the case. We might be completely wrong about the Lord's will or need to await His timing or need to learn something He wants to teach us.

In those situations we live by faith, and our faith sustains us. We give thanks; we keep walking; we keep praying; and we keep listening. We cannot give up because our God will never forsake us.

The experience with Lisa was a stunning miracle. I do not know why that prayer of desperation was answered so decisively, while another prayer of desperation, one that had lasted my lifetime, seemed only to fall back into my lap unheard.

That was the prayer for help in the painful and strained relationship with my earthly father.

God was equally merciful in both situations. So why, even on the other side of the world from my parents' little house in California, did that relationship remain one of the most challenging areas of prayer for me? I am not sure that I will understand it all in this lifetime. But, by God's grace, I was at last about to find peace.

10

PEACE AT LAST

Then, the same day at evening, being the first day of the week,
when the doors were shut where the disciples were assembled,
for fear of the Jews, Jesus came and stood in the midst, and
said to them, "Peace be with you."

John 20:19 NKJV

We completed the year of Bible school—it had passed
so quickly—and were now living in the beautiful city
of Christchurch on the South Island of New Zealand.

We remembered the particular beauty of New Zealand
from our earlier mission work, but were taken aback by it
nonetheless. We were *oohing* and *aahing* continually. It was
February when we arrived, summer there, and the grass was
greener, the skies bluer, the flowers more vibrant—everything
crystal clean and clear. I have noticed since then, on flights
into that country, that there is a mighty intake of breath by

the airline passengers who are peering out the windows as the jet descends.

After completing our courses at New Life Bible School, David was asked by the senior pastor of New Life Centre, Peter Morrow, to stay a while longer in order to teach in some neighboring cities. This led eventually to his becoming a part of the senior leadership at the church as well as at the Bible school.

David was also being drawn into an itinerate teaching ministry, being asked more and more frequently to speak at meetings in people's homes in the rural areas around Christchurch. The farmers who gathered together expressed a great deal of appreciation that someone from the church would come and teach them. Many of these wonderful people would then come to the services the next Sunday. We soon realized that the Lord was using this ministry to grow the church.

We had settled into a nice apartment on the grounds of the Bible school. Lisa and Tina were happy in the local elementary school just a couple of blocks away. All seemed to be going well.

But I was not at peace.

Each day I grew more distressed and guilty that we had not returned to the mission field of New Guinea. We knew that our successors had seen the church-building project through to the end, but we had talked with them as well as some of the missionary leaders in Port Moresby about possibly returning. David felt released from this, but I had a nagging ache that we should keep our word.

Now another winter was approaching. The June frosts sparkled like crystal on the chilled ground most mornings. At night, even though I was tired after such busy days, I lay awake praying and staring at the moonlight beaming through the sheer curtains onto the bedroom floor.

One such night, as I thought about New Guinea, tears began spilling out of my eyes. David slept peacefully, assured that we were in the right place. I loved New Zealand, but I could not shake the gloom. I prayed and finally fell asleep after about two hours.

The next night, the same thing happened. And the third night. I did not know what to do but pray. I felt exhausted after weeping for three nights. It always surprised me that David was such a sound sleeper!

This third night my eyes were still full of tears, but through the blur I could see someone coming down the hallway toward our bedroom. The person, wearing a long robe, was walking quietly and quickly. Even though the girls never got up in the middle of the night, I assumed it was Lisa coming to me for a drink of water.

I could see by the soft glow of moonlight that the figure walked soundlessly into our room. I spoke to Lisa and waited, but there was no response. I continued to stare at the window for some reason, but when she did not answer, I turned my head to look.

To my shock Jesus stood there. His brightness suddenly flooded the room. My eyes, instantly clear, went to His face. I stared into His eyes, which seemed to dance with life. It was as though they moved backward, as if traveling through eternity.

I formed this thought in my mind: *I want to look right into His complete face.* The Lord allowed me to search His face for several seconds, as He smiled at me.

Then, just that quickly, Jesus disappeared. It was as though someone had switched off the lights. I rolled onto my back and my hands went straight up into the air, up into the darkness that had been bright and shining only a moment before. I began to worship the Lord Jesus out loud.

Then I heard the Lord speaking to me in my heart. He said, *I know everything in your heart. Everything in your heart, I know!* This brought incredible comfort to me as my eyes readjusted to the soft light of moonbeams dancing in the darkness. I knew that He was not condemning us for not returning to Port Moresby. I felt released by my Lord, the living God.

I fell asleep instantly. The next morning, I told David that Jesus had come into our bedroom just a few hours before. He was amazed, just as I was.

We got up, dressed and took the girls to school after breakfast. It was another normal day, but my heart was happy and free.

That morning, a godly young woman whose bedroom was on the other side of ours stopped by for a visit. Before she left I told her about Jesus coming in the night, trusting that she would keep it in confidence. To my amazement she told me that she also could not sleep the night before. While she was lying in her bed in the dark of night, her whole room began to light up. She was amazed at the flood of light, which then gently receded.

She told me, "Nancy, Jesus must have gone through your wall and traveled right through my bedroom, lighting it up!" She was convinced of it.

All I could say was this: Jesus is indeed the *light* of the world. He comforts us in our weakness. He cheers us when we are sad. He answers our prayers, taking all our fears away. First Peter 5:7 offers such comfort, inviting us to "[cast] all your care upon Him, for He cares for you" (NKJV). Jesus might not always come to us in the way He came that night, but He is with us: "For He Himself has said, 'I will never leave you nor forsake you'" (Hebrews 13:5 NKJV).

Now that my heart was at peace, I was able to enjoy life in New Zealand. Peter encouraged us to stay yet another year because of the rapid growth in the church. Before long, David was brought on staff as principal of the Bible school. With this decision made, we were able to buy a house.

When we had been in New Zealand for three years, our third daughter was born. God Himself named this child. Soon after her birth, as the doctor handed the precious bundle to David, I heard the Lord say, *Her name is Debra.* I sensed the word *Joy* for her middle name.

It was soon after her birth that the Lord gave me peace in that most difficult and troubled area of my life—my relationship with my father.

The first time he saw his first grandchild, Lisa, he showed a softer side—something I had never seen before. Lisa had the likeness of his own round face, more like his Schultz side. His genuine love for the children brought a lot of solace to my grieved heart.

Once David and I began our life of mission work and lived in such faraway places, it was too expensive to communicate readily by phone. But I wrote him and my mother letters. She sent us letters and cards, and one time he wrote me back—one sheet on both sides. Whenever we were in the States we made short visits, and the girls were the highlight of our trips. There was a bit of healing that came through the years.

Then when Debra was about a year old, Leonard and Martha paid a small fortune—about ten thousand dollars—for

David and me and the three children to fly back to the States for a visit so the grandparents could see the newest addition to the family. Lisa was ten, and Tina seven.

We had planned to stay the first two weeks with my parents in the little house in Adelanto, but it was a disaster. They were not ready for us. Then after only three days, my father began saying that it cost too much for us to stay there; he told me that he and my mother wanted us to leave.

My life was a storm when I was with him. Deep down I loved my father, but I struggled to understand the rejection and pain of our relationship. I realized that as a child I had been the blockage of his mission plans. I was, simply put, in his way. Now that I was an adult, he would start shouting at me these puzzling words: "You have to love me!" I could only beg him to tell me why he was always so angry with me. Tears would wash away the sadness I felt. That and prayer were my only defenses. I truly wanted to have peace with my father.

We had to let Leonard and Martha know that we were coming a week and a half early, and they scrambled to be ready for us.

The last day of that ill-fated visit with my parents, we loaded the suitcases into our rental car and packed sandwiches for a final lunch in a park. After we had eaten, David stood up from the picnic table and said to my mother, "Let's take the girls for a walk."

My father and I remained seated. It was a beautiful day in June with blue skies. It was a peaceful setting—and an opportunity to talk. I began slowly.

"Daddy," I said, "can't we stay a little longer?"

He did not meet my eyes. "I can't pay for it."

"But, Daddy, it's embarrassing to go to the Ravenhills so quickly. Could we stay even a few days?"

He looked over at me. His voice was not loud, but it was harsh. "It's costing about a hundred dollars a day with all of you here. I don't have that kind of money."

This time I glanced away, looking at the trees and empty tables. The other picnickers had packed their belongings or gone to explore the grounds.

So he was worried about money. That seemed to be a constant with him—money and his health. We knew his liver was deteriorating. He had had liver problems all his life. And he was getting older, but I did not realize how sick he was.

He brought up the past, and the cycle of pain whirred around us once more. He argued; I wept. I sensed that I needed to ask his forgiveness in order to feel peace between us and to clear the air. After some moments he responded with those words that seemed incongruous with such a harsh delivery: "You've got to love me!"

But for the first time I realized what he was actually saying. He wanted to feel forgiven for the tempests of his life. Maybe he believed that the Lord had forgiven him, but in some fearful place in his heart he needed to hear that I held nothing against him.

"You've got to love me!" Again those words! His eyes flashed anger.

Truly, I was sick of the whole thing. I was 35 years old—and weary of a lifetime of grief. But more, I knew that God had allowed us this time together. We were meant to make things right. I wanted to leave with peace in my heart.

I took a quick breath and said with genuine conviction: "I love you, Daddy."

He turned away.

We sat in silence until the rest of the family ambled back to us. David and I then situated the children into the car, preparing to drive away. My father and I spoke few words. Something seemed settled in his attitude, an edge had softened.

After we returned to New Zealand, about a year after our visit to the States, the Lord gave me a word of promise. A visiting pastor was ministering at our church. One night, after he and David had been praying together, they came into the kitchen where I was reading Debra a story and this godly man spoke prophetically to us.

He looked at David and me and said, "God has given me a word for you two: All of your parents are going to die in peace. You have wondered, Nancy." Then he quoted wonderful encouraging Scriptures. He was right—I had wondered. Plus, I did not know what impact their deaths would have on me.

Two months later, my father dropped dead in his living room.

When my mother called to tell me, she said simply words that she had told me before: "Daddy mellowed, Nancy."

This time I chose to believe that it was true because of the way he had been with my children and because of his sincere desire throughout his life to serve the Lord. I also wanted things to be peaceable. I wanted to believe the best about him.

I was not able to fly back for the funeral, but I thought about his being in heaven. I had died once, and knew that everything was beautiful there. I thought how after death, you are complete. You do not have the mind issues, the bitterness.

And you have a spiritual body—the people I saw were dressed. I remembered how my own body had felt light and unencumbered concerning earthly things.

I knew that, inside, he was now completely whole in Jesus. I can look forward to seeing him again because he will be healed—not only healed physically, but also healed from his lifelong search for unconditional love.

There is power in surrender—in the sense of giving our pain to Jesus. This is not weakness; it is being like our Savior who, in His strength, was also meek. It is a place of trust and peace. The Spirit of God can do that within our hearts. Life is hard enough to get through without holding on to chains from the past. I embraced the peace that God had promised me.

I do not know why it was harder to walk in that peace when my mother died three years later from stomach cancer.

She had called me in New Zealand one day and told me that she was alone and probably not going to live much longer. I left the children with David and made the long trip back. I stayed with her for about two months, but finally had to return home.

I felt terrible about leaving her, and she died one week later. As with my father, I could not attend her funeral. David was able to travel to California afterward and get her little house ready for sale.

Even though I knew that she was in heaven and that I would see her again, I suffered from the loss. My skin broke out, and I scratched the rash until it was raw. Sometimes in the middle of the night I would fill the tub and soak in bath salts, hoping for relief for my mind as well as my body. It felt as though the bottom had dropped out.

After about a month, I wrote everyone who knew my parents, saying that they were both now with the Lord and completely healed. I wrote about how glorious it must be for them to be in heaven and with Jesus. With that declaration in writing, I could love and release them both.

11

EARLY MORNING WITH JESUS

Now on the first day of the week Mary Magdalene came early to the tomb, while it was still dark, and saw the stone already taken away from the tomb. . . . [The angels] said to her, "Woman, why are you weeping?" She said to them, "Because they have taken away my Lord, and I do not know where they have laid Him." . . . She turned around and saw Jesus standing there, and did not know that it was Jesus.

John 20:1, 13–14

From the earliest times that Jesus appeared to me, He wore a long white robe. And in eternity I saw Him robed and seated on a magnificent golden throne.

In Kansas, He met me wearing casual slacks and a jacket! Why this unusual occurrence? Let me explain how this extraordinary appearance came about.

During the thirteen years that we lived in New Zealand as part of New Life Centre, God led us to move eight times. Buying and selling eight houses in that time frame was nothing short of a miracle. Daily I would get down on the floor on my stomach and pray. I had to stay close to the Lord considering what we were doing.

Then I would hear the Lord say, *It is time to get out of this house*, and we would know it was time to relocate. David never questioned these directives. He and the other pastors would meet to talk and pray about where we should live next.

This unusual service to God grew out of the speaking ministry that David was called to from the time we moved to New Zealand. Just as he had gone into the farmers' homes in the immediate area surrounding Christchurch to teach and minister, so now he continued to do so as we moved from suburb to suburb. He visited homes and held meetings in the public schools on Sunday nights.

It was not easy, but we were willing to relocate our family and reach out to the community as our contribution to the pastoral teamwork. The other associate pastors conducted meetings on Sunday nights as well, and it was astounding how the church grew. New Life Centre was based in the beautiful old Majestic Theatre downtown, which had been remodeled. With the congregation spreading out, other churches began springing up around the city.

We were committed to our work and the people in New Zealand, but the day came when the Lord guided us to return to the United States.

Thus, in February 1988 we arrived in a suburb of Dallas, Texas, to be near his parents, and sought the Lord's further direction. David spent most of that year on his face, praying in an office he constructed in our garage. It was wonderful that we could see Leonard and Martha each week. They lived about one hundred miles away from us.

Lisa began attending Texas Women's University in Denton, and Tina enrolled at Christ For The Nations Bible School in Dallas. I had hoped that in the States we could all stay together, but David, Debra and I were soon moving once again.

David and I had been invited to join the pastoral team of Kansas City Fellowship in Kansas City, Missouri, under senior pastor Mike Bickle. David was offered the pastorate of a wonderful church in neighboring Olathe, Kansas. This was one of the six churches in the area that comprised the fellowship.

It was painful to leave the two girls behind us in Dallas, but we obeyed the Lord's word to us. We moved to Olathe and rented a lovely home soon after our arrival. It was in this location that Jesus made such an unusual appearance.

Our neighborhood sat amid small hills, which were topped here and there with wooded patches of large and magnificent trees. Blacktopped paths sloped down from the back doors of the houses to various jogging trails.

One flawless morning in May, I awoke early and decided to get up and exercise. I was certain to be ahead of the other joggers, so with barely a glance in the mirror, I threw on some old clothes in order to go and return quickly before taking Debra to school. Then, later in the day, a friend was coming by to give me some pointers on how to wear my hair and change my makeup. It was bothering me that I was looking much older. This was part of what impelled me to get up and exercise so early that morning.

I left the house and ran down to the park, where I pounded the blacktopped path for about a mile, praying about the day ahead.

Then I turned and headed back. As I was running near the open field, I noticed a grove of tall trees in the distance. I said to myself, *I don't remember seeing that grouping of trees before. They're so beautiful!*

My eyes then focused on a man standing near the tall trees looking out in the direction of the field. His clothes were white and his hood was draped loosely over his head. I noticed this because most joggers who wore their hoods up usually tied them snugly.

I said to myself, *Oh, no! I didn't want to see anyone out here today. My hair must look just awful!*

As I got closer to him, I could see light coming from his face, and it amazed me. I knew somehow that he was saying to himself, as he looked out across the field, the words *This is good.*

Up close I saw that he was wearing loose-fitting slacks and a matching jacket. It looked like beautiful material. Everything about him seemed to exude joy and energy.

Some of his gladness seemed to pull joy from within me. Planning to pass him by without speaking, I instead put on a big smile and said, "Hi!"

He looked at me—and I knew.

His expression then changed to sadness. I shrank inside because I realized He could see me within. I also felt great love in my inner person, and a desire to talk once again with my earthly father.

The sadness melted in His radiant smile. "Did you warm it up for Me out there today?" He asked.

I looked at Him and said, "Yep!" This word I never use popped cheerily out of my mouth.

As this exchange was taking place, I began to feel as if I were running in slow motion. My feet were as light as those of a leaping deer. He turned toward me, and the light I had seen coming from His face seemed to blaze like a laser beam right into my head. Time stopped.

Then He spoke without physically forming words with His mouth. Out of the stillness and silence, I heard three sentences:

Do you know who I really am?

Do you know who you really are?

The body is just a shell.

I tried to stop myself, but it took another leap or two. When I turned around, He was not there. I strained to look in every direction. I ran two more steps, turned around again and stood, looking down the path, but no Man was there.

Though I saw no one, I now could hear men's voices in conversation over my head. I managed to comprehend that these were angels—and they were discussing me! "She doesn't know what to do next. . . . She wonders where He has gone. . . . Will she go home or keep looking for Him?" They were following my progress.

Debra needed to go to school so I kept going, but I was shaken. I had just seen the Lord Jesus, Son of Man, Son of God.

I could hardly believe it. What was I to make of this supernatural visit? I walked mechanically through the day, pondering this Man and His words to me.

Do you know who I really am?

These words have not stopped ringing in my heart. Who really understands the Son of God? And yet the Bible tells us who He is.

He is God Almighty, maker of heaven and earth. The King of kings and Lord of lords. He is the God I worship and praise, and the God I live to please.

Psalm 150 ends with the words, "Let everything that has breath praise the LORD. Praise the LORD!" Psalm 144:5, 7 says, "Bow Your heavens, O LORD, and come down! . . . Stretch forth Your hand from on high; rescue me and deliver me."

He is the Creator who loves His creation. This is fundamental. But do I really know Him?

He was prodding my thinking. *Who am I? How do I operate in your life? You need to know Me.*

It raised for me the question of how I use my time, as this can be a good indicator of commitment.

Am I a good disciple? Like most people, I love my freedom. And with David traveling so much I could be far too interested in sitting back watching television. But He promises that His yoke is easy in the work of the Kingdom. He takes the burden. The Kingdom is on His shoulders. As the old hymn adjures us, we must work for the night is coming. We do not have the option of sitting around being lazy.

The book of Hebrews gives a powerful definition of who Jesus is:

God, who at various times and in various ways spoke in time past to the fathers by the prophets, has in these last days spoken to us by His Son, whom He has appointed heir of all things, through whom also He made the worlds; who being the brightness of His glory and the express image of His person, and upholding all things by the word of His power, when He had by Himself purged our sins, sat down at the right hand of the Majesty on high.

To the Son He says: "Your throne, O God, is forever and ever; a scepter of righteousness is the scepter of Your kingdom. . . . God, Your God, has anointed You with the oil of gladness more than Your companions." And: "You, LORD, in the beginning laid the foundation of the earth, and the heavens are the work of Your hands. They will perish, but You remain; and they will all grow old like a garment . . . but You are the same."

Hebrews 1:1–3; 8–12 NKJV

Jesus made the universe. He is the brightness of the Father's glory, the very expression of His Father, upholding all things by the word of His power. The physical things will perish, but He and—by His mercy—"the children whom God has given [Him]" (Hebrews 2:13 NKJV) will remain.

Down the ages, God spoke to the prophets; He must have spoken to these people so they knew what to speak or write. It is not such an odd thing that He would visit people.

But we cannot make it happen.

I never expect these visits. I am more surprised than anybody. I think that is possibly why God told me ahead of time that He would be visiting me in my lifetime—so I would not be afraid of it.

I do not know that I will ever see Him again. I cannot make Him come. I usually think, *When will You come back?* And when He does come, and then disappears just as quickly, I always wish that He would stay longer.

His second question was an eye-opener for me.

Do you know who you really are?

I have felt for most of my life that the answer to this is: I am weak, fearful, helpless and inadequate. If God could come to me when I was five years old, I should have been bolder throughout my life. I have been too weak in my mind. I should have realized this and had greater faith. I should not have been fearful my whole life.

So many *should*s!

But, I know that through prayer I can overcome anything or anyone through the mighty power of Jesus. The shed blood of Jesus, His Word and mighty name are my weapons.

> For the weapons of our warfare are not carnal, but mighty in God for pulling down strongholds, casting down arguments and every high thing that exalts itself against the knowledge of God, bringing every thought into captivity to the obedience of Christ.
>
> 2 Corinthians 10:4–5 NKJV

Too often we doubt the revelation of God's Word about us—who we are, what we are supposed to do. We shrink back. If we truly believed how close He is, we could be healed or walk in the wisdom and authority that we need in order to do His will.

Hebrews 4:14 tells of our great High Priest who has passed through the heavens—Jesus, the Son of God. Let us hold fast our profession so we can live the godly lives He wants us to live. We are supposed to portray Him. Do we? We are supposed to be holy in this godless world. Are we? It is revelation that changes us by the Holy Spirit and helps us accomplish these things.

What is revelation? It is knowing what God really wants me to do with my life. If I knew this with assurance, I would not disobey. That is revelation, and that is what I want.

The body is just a shell.

Years ago when we first arrived in New Zealand, I went often with David to his speaking engagements to help out. One night our discussion group was asked to consider what we feared most in life.

I knew instantly: I was afraid to die. Even though I had entered eternity and seen dear relatives who were in heaven— and even though I had seen Jesus looking at me with such love—still I realized that I had fear in my heart.

Everyone in the group that night spoke out his or her fears. I said, "I'm afraid to die." Immediately, the man leading the meeting turned to me and quoted Hebrews 2:14–15. The Lord quickened it to him with great authority:

> Inasmuch then as the children have partaken of flesh and blood, He Himself likewise shared in the same, that through death He might destroy him who had the power of death, that is, the devil, and release those who through fear of death were all their lifetime subject to bondage.
>
> NKJV

When I heard those words from Scripture that night, I knew I was released from the fear of death.

So why was Jesus talking to me about the body?

He was telling me not to worry so much about how I look because that is based in fear. This has always been a challenge for me because I felt so ugly as a child. I accepted ugliness as fact. I had no confidence.

Jesus wanted to get me out of self-consciousness. It can be consuming to try to live up to images that we feel are acceptable.

In other words, *What is really necessary in life?*

We all deal with this balance every day, sometimes forgetting our appearance and other times spending too much time on the outer shell.

God was showing His great love for you and me in His words about the body. Spiritual insight is the higher calling.

He does not want us to miss all that He longs to give us simply because we are focused on the wrong things.

Granted, there can be purity in looking nice.

When I saw Jesus in eternity, there was a band of gold in the fabric around His neck, a band of gold at His waist and a band of gold several inches wide at the bottom of His white robe. That is the only time I have seen Him when He was literally sparkling. And He was sitting on that beautiful huge throne of pure gold.

This tells me that there is a time and a place for physical beauty for us, too.

Psalm 45, the lovely wedding song, describes a scene of human grandeur, addressing first the Bridegroom, then the Bride:

> Kings' daughters are among Your honorable women: at Your right hand stands the queen in gold from Ophir.
>
> Listen, O daughter, consider and incline your ear; forget your own people also, and your father's house: so the King will greatly desire your beauty; because He is your Lord, worship Him. . . . The royal daughter is all glorious within the palace; her clothing is woven with gold. She shall be brought to the King in robes of many colors; the virgins, her companions who follow her, shall be brought to You. With gladness and rejoicing they shall be brought; they shall enter the King's palace.
>
> Verses 9–11, 13–15 NKJV

The solution is to do our best with the physical, but not to focus too much on it. There is a balance. The Holy Spirit will show us if we are crossing a line. Besides, there is only so much we can do; ultimately, gravity takes over!

For the next three days after Jesus spoke these words to me, I did not sleep well. I lay awake at night, wondering about this experience. On the third night, as I lay still, I felt a hand on my forehead touching me lightly. I said out loud in the dark, "Lord, was that You in the park this week?"

I heard in my heart His words back to me, *Yes, Nancy.*

Then I finally fell asleep.

The supernatural is real. Jesus is with us. And He cares.

12

A HARD GOOD-BYE

"Truly, truly, I say to you, you will weep and lament, but the world will rejoice. You will grieve, but your grief will be turned into joy."

John 16:20

After four years serving with Kansas City Fellowship, David and I received a call from a Vineyard church to come and minister in Washington State. The offer of senior pastor was a great opportunity to put into practice everything we had learned in New Zealand and Kansas City.

So we were on the move again.

David took charge at the church, and we began to see the attendance grow. I led the women's program. We had prayer meetings, Bible studies, counseling, and women's conferences when special speakers would come in for weekends. Debra came with us and lived at home while she attended junior college in Tacoma.

We lived on the Puget Sound, which is stunningly beautiful, in the little fishing village of Gig Harbor. Mount Rainier is an active volcano and can be seen in the distance on most days. David and I would say to each other, "I can't believe God brought us to this amazing place!" When the mist came down in the mornings, it brought a dreamy kind of feeling all over town. At those times, Mount Rainier was shrouded in swirls of clouds and rain.

But in the midst of the many exciting things the Lord was doing, He showed me again through a great loss in my life that He is always near. In November 1994 Leonard became quite sick. When he was hospitalized, we knew the end was near.

I always marveled at God's goodness to put me into a family where I could experience what it was like to have a godly father who had both strength and mercy.

I remember Leonard telling me about meekness one time. He was driving me to the airport, and I was telling him about someone who was getting under my skin.

He listened and then said, "Nancy, have you ever seen those big machines that come down like big jaws and crush things?"

I nodded.

"Well," he said, "some of them are so sensitive they can crack a nutshell. That's what meekness is all about. Meekness is the most powerful and finely tuned tool you have. If you listen to the Holy Spirit, you can just forgive and go on."

Leonard exhibited meekness. In the pulpit he was like a lion, but at home or in person he was like a lamb. He did not have to prove anything to anybody. He was a powerhouse, but was as sensitively tuned to the voice of the Holy Spirit as anyone I have ever known.

I remember the last time we said good-bye at the door of his house. I was dashing off to catch a plane in Dallas to get back to Gig Harbor, and my ride was waiting out front.

Leonard was unsteady on his feet and weak. I turned at the front door and looked at him, saying, "I hope I see you again, Len."

He came to me and gave me a kiss on the cheek. Then with a big twinkle in his eye, he said, "So do I!"

I knew what he meant: *I will be in heaven.*

I answered with a smile, but felt hit in the stomach. I hated to leave. I turned and hurried down the path to the waiting car, thinking, *Don't look back.*

David and I went to Texas for the funeral that November, and we saw many old friends, plus famous people who came to honor Leonard, and also relatives we would not see again. I needed to return to Washington the next morning, but David stayed with his mother for another three days.

A friend drove me to the airport, and we prayed together before she dropped me off. I boarded the plane and sat on the left side, by the window. A young man took the aisle seat, leaving a seat between us. I did not say anything to him, and he did not speak to me.

As I sat at the window, a horrible, incredible sadness draped over my soul like a pall. It hit me that Leonard was now with the Lord. Not only would we miss him terribly, but he would not be on earth praying for his children night and day. How we would miss his insight, wisdom and intimacy with the Lord! I sat motionless, staring out the window as the engines roared and the jet took off.

At that time, airlines offered a variety of refreshments. When the stewardess rolled her cart by us, the young man a seat over chatted with her, and handed me exactly what I wanted, though I had not said a word. The stewardess seemed to enjoy conversing with him and paused whenever she walked by to exchange a few pleasant words.

My mind was finally distracted from its sadness by this winsome young man. There was something unusual about him. Shortly before we landed, I asked the Lord if I could look at him, and as soon as I prayed, he turned his face toward me to look out the window at the clouds below us.

He was a short individual, and he had marks on his skin, as though perhaps a skin condition had left scarring. There was a sense of quietness about him that made the tears in my eyes want to spill over. Then my vision "adjusted." I saw him with new eyes. I saw what he really looked like.

Far from having a skin condition, his face was flawless. His beauty was stunning. My "radar" had been telling me for a few minutes that he was an angel, and this was confirmed by the sight of his extraordinary visage.

I did not speak to him or acknowledge this, or even feel that it was unusual. In the way of supernatural things, I simply accepted it.

Then the Lord gave me a message of comfort. Supernatural events are not usually heralded by trumpets. Events that might be explained as ordinary could easily be orchestrated for us by the Lord. (We will talk more about angelic "coincidences" in the next chapter.)

Take, for instance, what happened next. I had been listening about this time to a minister on television who told how believers are like runners in a race, moving steadily toward a finish line as we seek to please God and do His will. He told the story of the ancient Greek messenger who ran to Athens with news of success in battle, shouting, *Nike!* (meaning "triumph" or "victory"). He said the practice was taken up by ancient runners and that, like them, we should be able to shout *Nike!* at the end—"Victory!" It was a teaching that touched my heart.

The words of that sermon came to me now. I knew that Leonard had ended his race full of energy and spirit. I could imagine him yelling *Nike!* as he leapt victorious over the finish line.

When the plane came to a stop and the door was opened, I gathered my belongings in preparation for joining the queue of travelers inching slowly up the aisle. People stood and opened the overhead bins to pull down their belongings, and lumbered along pleasantly. The young man reached down under the seat in front of him and grabbed an amazingly long, thick bag. I had not seen him shove it under there and wondered how it had ever fit.

The big letters stitched along the side caught my eye: *Nike.* The young man glanced at me. Then, lifting the bag over his shoulder, he slid into the crowd and out of sight. He simply disappeared. I have never seen anyone deplane like that, right through the mob of people. It was as Genesis 24:40 says: "He said to me, 'The Lord, before whom I have walked, will send His angel with you to make your journey successful.'"

Then God spoke to my heart as I watched the disappearing form with the Nike bag: *Leonard triumphed, Nancy! He won the victory. He is with the Lord. Be thankful. Be happy, because he is rejoicing. He is in glory with Jesus. Now, you take up the baton and go forward, rejoicing. You and David still have work to do!*

When I think of that experience and look forward to seeing Leonard again, my mind goes to 1 Thessalonians:

> But we do not want you to be uninformed, brethren, about those who are asleep, so that you will not grieve as do the rest who have no hope. . . . For the Lord himself will descend from heaven with a shout, with the voice of the archangel and with the trumpet of God and the dead in Christ will rise first. Then we who are alive and remain will be caught up together with them in the clouds to meet the Lord in the air, and so we shall always be with the Lord.
>
> 1 Thessalonians 4:13, 16–17

Until that glorious day, we are directed by Scripture to draw near to God as we work for the Kingdom, trusting that He will in turn draw near to us (see James 4:8).

How do we go about this? We look with the eyes of faith. Faith takes its stand on the Word of God and dares to claim the promises written there as its own. By believing "that He is" and "that He is a rewarder of those who seek Him" (Hebrews 11:6), we can enter His presence boldly (see Hebrews 4:16).

David and I made the decision to be happy for Leonard's homegoing, but I cannot say that it was easy. We would no longer see Leonard on this earth, but our heavenly Father was as close as ever, and we found great comfort in that.

13

WAYS THAT ANGELS MINISTER TO US

The angel of the LORD encamps around those who fear Him,
and rescues them.

Psalm 34:7

It is a curious thing that angels—who in their world are
majestic, robed, winged creatures—can walk around earth
like ordinary human beings. Maybe we expect angels to appear in a blaze of radiance. After all, the apostle Paul calls
them "ministers of fire." But they also can walk among us
undetected; we can be unaware of them. Unless God lifts the
veil from our eyes, we will not realize that we have experienced
something supernatural.

If the Lord had not shown me a different reality on that
flight after Leonard's funeral, for instance, I might have
thought that the young man's Nike bag was an extraordinary

coincidence. A perfectly normal piece of luggage owned by a perfectly normal human being.

In this chapter I want to share with you several ways that angels minister to us. The Lord brought these particular supernatural encounters with the angelic into my view for a reason. I hope that they will encourage you to believe that God is at work in the "ordinary" experiences of your life.

Here, then, shown in the stories that follow, are five of the many ways that angels minister to us:

They give help when we are in distress.
They confirm the Lord's guidance.
They assure us of His presence.
They deliver messages from heaven.
They remind us of God's love.

Help in Distress

It seemed when we lived in Washington State that I was constantly being called for jury duty. On a dark misty morning near the end of two weeks on a particular case, I arrived at the courthouse, went through the gate to the lot and looked desperately for a parking place. Round and round I went— and finally spotted one. I gunned the engine, slid into the space and rushed into the courtroom.

There we jurors sat, listening dutifully to the presentation of evidence. At lunchtime, I thought I would take the opportunity to tell two of the other jurors, who I knew were not believers, about our wonderful God. It seemed like a good time to share my faith, but I did not get a good response.

A wall came up between us. The women muttered a stiff reply and avoided walking beside me as we returned to the courtroom.

That afternoon, with a laugh from the judge who cited preposterous evidence, the case was thrown out. We were finally released. The two weeks spent in the courtroom now seemed like a dreadful waste of time. I was still smarting from the responses of the other jurors to my attempt to share about Jesus. And the final plunge of my emotions came when I returned to my car and discovered that the battery was dead. I had left the lights on all day.

The other drivers in the parking lot were hurrying on their way out the gate and into the gathering darkness. I had no phone, and soon I was left alone.

I began to pray.

After a few minutes, I opened my eyes to see a white sport utility vehicle coming slowly in my direction. It pulled beside me and a man and his little boy, who was about seven, climbed out. Tall and blond, they looked to be Scandinavian and were dressed in white slacks.

Tears of gratitude filled my eyes. *God,* I said, *You have met my need.*

The Holy Spirit told me not to say anything to them or offer any money for their service; just observe. Though they looked like any father and son, I knew that this was the hand of God and did as He had directed.

The man said simply, "You need help."

I opened my trunk and pulled out a set of jumper cables. "I need to get this car going." That was all either of us said.

The man barely looked at me as he connected the cables. I got into my car and turned the key. The engine jumped to life.

With a simple thank you, I took the cables from his hand and put them back into my trunk. He and the boy got into their car and drove toward the gate.

I was so relieved and so grateful tears filled my eyes.

I put the car into gear and came up behind the white SUV at the exit gate, trying to pull my wrought nerves together. As the driver completed his transaction and pulled away, his license plate caught my attention. It began to dance and glisten with light. It was practically popping with electricity. Then the numbers and letters registered with me. It had my initials—NR—followed by the numerals—month, day and year—of my birth date. The car drove through the gate and was gone.

The ticket collector must have wondered what was wrong with me. I was crying my eyes out. Those angels must have come down from heaven for me.

Confirmation of His Guidance

I believe that God is more "hands on" than we realize, or-chestrating His angelic visitations to intersect our lives. Even if we falter or miss His leading, He can see to it that we are in the right place at the appointed time. Or He can confirm that we are on the right track.

This was the case when the Lord nudged us to move from Washington State.

I have heard David preach many times on the life of Abra-ham. One particular message was titled, "The Altar, the Tent and the Well." David explained how the minute God said, "Move on," Abraham would roll up his tent and go. When he got to the appointed place, he would make an altar and then dig another well.

That is the obedience God wants in His people. When difficult times come or if something traumatic happens or if He asks us to give up something we love, we need to be flexible enough to pick up and go on again.

Sometimes this is not so easy. David and I have endeavored to pack up and follow Him, the Lamb of God, wherever He leads us. But it was particularly hard to leave Gig Harbor. We really loved our church and the area and wanted to stay, but God had other plans for our lives. After five years of pastoring the Vineyard Church there, we realized that He was giving us new marching orders.

Through various means, God made it clear that He wanted us in Florida. We had bought a house by this time and put it on the market. We made two or three trips to Pensacola before buying a home and resettling there. We were going only out of obedience, wondering how we would build an altar to the Lord in this new place.

One day during this process I had some free time and decided to go for a walk. I wandered down our road and up a hill to a housing development that was rather desolate. Deer milled among the flowers and fir trees. The Puget Sound was visible from the edge of the hillside, with the ferries churning the waters around the dock at Tacoma. It was a lovely place to walk and pray.

On the left-hand side of the road, farther back and away from the road, was a brand-new house. I had watched it being built whenever I walked down this hillside.

As I turned to head for home, I could not help but notice a large truck parked in front of the house. It was painted deep red and looked new. I smiled when I saw it because my maiden name—Schultz—was printed in large letters across the hood. A logo on the side of the truck identified Schultz Construction. While the name Schultz was everywhere present back in my childhood home of St. Joseph, it was unusual in this part of the country.

The more I thought about it, the more I wondered if this unusual sight was possibly a divine appointment confirming our plans to move. That evening I told David about my experience. He suggested I go back to the house the next day and ask the man living there if he had hired that company.

I was hesitant to do this, fearful of what the man might think, but the next day I walked back up the road to the house. When I knocked, a friendly elderly man opened the door. I told him where I lived, and he invited me to come in. So I did.

His first words were, "I've just paid off every bill on this new house!" He was so happy. He said he had no family, but was going to live there by himself.

I asked about the red truck the day before, but he said he had not used any individual or company with that name in building his house. Nor had he seen the truck.

We chatted a bit more and soon I was walking back home, wondering why God had given me such an unusual experience. I could not prove anything, but I was certain that God had done it to confirm the next step of our journey.

That evening, while relaying the adventure to David, I heard God speaking to me. This is what He said: *I know it isn't easy always to leave your church, your home, your friends, your family. Trust Me, Nancy, because I know what I'm doing and what I plan to do with your lives. You are "under construction" and I'm the construction manager! Just obey Me. Trust*

Me. All will be well. You are on a pilgrimage, a journey, even as Abraham and Sarah were. They had to travel throughout the land—being uprooted, living in tents, digging wells and building altars again and again. They obeyed Me whenever I told them to go.

Sometimes disappointments are really God's appointments. We can be sad about a turn of events, but God is always working in our lives to take us a different way or teach us something new. He is closing a door or opening a door, as the book of Revelation teaches.

So like Abraham and Sarah, David and I picked up our tent once again and readied ourselves to move to the Emerald Coast. The Lord was leading us to take part in the revival that had just broken out in the Brownsville Assembly of God. The pastoral staff had asked David to take one of the instructor positions at the new Bible school. It had formed quickly and already had 1,800 students when we arrived.

Assurance of His Presence

Much had happened in our family over the previous years. Lisa had entered the mission field and was working with an organization in Kunming, China. Tina had married, and she and George would soon be welcoming their fourth child into the family. Debra was living with Tina and George in Colorado Springs while doing her student teaching. It would be only a few years before she would meet and marry Jarrod, and they would begin raising their four children in New Zealand.

In the midst of these busy days, Lisa came home for Christmas to help us dismantle our lives and resettle in Florida.

Leaving the snowy Northwest in midwinter, the three of us made the long drive south to sunshine and palm trees to begin life anew.

Our house in Pensacola was located about thirty minutes from the large Brownsville church. Revival had broken out in 1995, about two years before our arrival. As word spread of God's healing presence abiding there, people flew into Pensacola daily from around the world.

The pain of leaving our wonderful church in Gig Harbor was now a memory. I realized that I might be in Pensacola for the rest of my life, so I worked hard to adjust to the new lifestyle of church meetings almost every night. It was wonderful to see God touching lives with His healing power, His forgiveness. We rejoiced as the glory of God came upon people as they repented and cried out to Him for more of His Presence.

After about two weeks, Lisa needed to return to China to resume her missionary work. Early on the appointed day of her flight, we packed her luggage in the car, marveling at the unusual fog. Cold morning air was dipping and rolling over the warm Florida earth, and the resultant creamy mist swirled around our neighborhood streets.

I sat in the backseat with Lisa in order to chat with her more easily, and also to take advantage of being close to her before she left us once again. It was hard to send her off on such a long and difficult journey by herself.

David eased the car out of our driveway moving at a snail's pace in the fog.

About one block from our house, Lisa and I turned to look out the back window and saw an amazing sight. Coming down our road behind us was a large man, slightly overweight, in nothing less than a tuxedo. His shirt looked freshly starched, and he wore a top hat and shiny two-tone shoes. With his walking stick, he looked like someone from a century ago.

He walked jauntily along behind our car, easily keeping up as we rolled forward. We were amused that he looked so very British. We could even distinguish his waxed mustache.

With her eyes on this unusual character, Lisa burst out, "Dad, this is an angel!"

David, glancing into the rearview mirror, was less sure. "It must be someone in costume out for a stroll," he suggested. But Lisa and I laughed good-naturedly in protest of this idea. As we peered out the back window, the gentleman continued smiling at us, and when our car gradually picked up speed and drove away, he tipped his hat.

I believe that he was given to us as a sign of assurance that God would watch over Lisa that week on her long journey to southwest China. I believed Him that day—and she arrived safely.

Messages from Heaven

David and I continued attending meetings at Brownsville almost every night of the week, but before long David's work shifted. As it turned out, he taught at the Bible school for only a couple of months. First he was asked to speak at the large Awake America crusades that grew out of the revival. Along with this, many individuals who came to Pensacola from various countries around the world asked him to come and speak in their churches.

It was evident that God was opening door after door, launching David into full-time traveling ministry.

I grew ever prouder of him as this ministry grew. He was following in the footsteps of his father—pastoring, praying, writing books, carrying the Gospel message all over the world. Our name is one I feel blessed to own.

Yet while this was a time of promotion for David, it was a valley for me. It was a time of deeper discipline, accented by aloneness, even within a very busy schedule. It was our prayer that this season would produce God's power, positioning and eternal purpose in both our lives.

I rarely joined David at the Awake America crusades, but the opportunity to attend one in Niagara Falls presented itself and I was thrilled.

The most cost effective way for me to fly to New York meant traveling on Saturday. All of the people involved with Awake America would be arriving Sunday evening. David was coming from Canada, where he was speaking that weekend, and would arrive on Sunday evening as well.

My flight was uneventful. I made my way to our hotel late Saturday night by taxi. The next morning I sat in a restaurant booth, eating breakfast and wondering how to spend the day.

The obvious excursion was to see the falls so I got directions from the waitress. As I headed out the door I was surprised at the cold on such a bright sunny day. But then I remembered I was not in Florida.

A ten-minute walk brought me to the Niagara River and a grassy park where I could sit on a bench and look at the bubbly river as it raced to the incredible falls. Mist ascended from the raging waters as they poured over the rocky edge.

I decided to take the bridge across the Niagara River and then roamed through the woods on the other side. People seemed to spill out from all directions and fill the park. There was beauty everywhere. I should have been enjoying myself—but I could not shake the sense of isolation that hovered over me in this difficult season of my life. I pictured myself during those difficult days in the words of Psalm 102:7: "I have become like a lonely bird on a housetop."

I was thinking my gloomy thoughts when three people walked toward me. Two men were on either side of a woman who was rather short and slightly overweight. She was dressed in a beautiful yellow suit and wore heels. Everyone else there that day seemed to be dressed casually—mostly in jeans. She turned her head from side to side, looking into the faces of her companions as they strolled along.

The threesome caught my eye because they walked abreast on the sidewalk and seemed to be having the time of their lives. They were chatting and laughing as they strolled along, often linking arms.

That was not the only time I saw them. As I wandered about through the day, I saw them everywhere—on a bench, down a path, in a shop. I was not trying to be near them; they simply seemed always to be in view.

At one point I was about half a block behind them as the sun shone down through the trees. The light seemed to dance all over the back of the woman's suit. There was fun and joy all around me that day, but I had never in my life felt so alone.

The trio stopped. In order to keep walking I had to pass them. A crowd bumbled alongside us about that time, and I drew myself up to slide past.

At that moment one of the two men turned toward me and spoke. He said, "It's not easy to be alone, to have your husband away so much of the time, but God sees sacrifice and He knows."

His words soaked into the dry depths of my heart. Those few words were a message from God. He was speaking through this messenger.

The thought came to me of a time many years earlier when I was just six years old and God spoke to me through a picture. Our home in St. Joseph, where Jesus first came to me, was on Price Street. One night after a severe whipping, I was praying. I was telling God that I wanted to be with Him every day of my life. It was a child's prayer of commitment to service, and I meant it.

Then He showed me a picture of our house address and said, *It is not an accident that you live on Price Street. You will pay a price to live the life you want.*

As the tears of pain and resolve flowed, I nodded and said simply, "Okay."

I had not known as a child what the price would be in order to live the life I desired—the price of never being able to stay in one place, never being able to keep anything of value, always being uprooted from family and friends, being alone so much.

Now, this evening in the beautiful park, I nodded once again at His message of encouragement. There was comfort simply in the fact that He knew.

I watched the trio until they were out of sight. God had given me a message through those happy "people." I knew that I had experienced Him.

Reminders of God's Love

I have little doubt that the abuse in my childhood battered my soul. So many years of pain leave you hurt. They take your confidence. But I never have given up believing that He loves me and will truly heal me.

Still, I continued to struggle for many more months in that valley of aloneness.

One day I went for a walk, choosing a road near our home that I knew to be isolated. I was lost in my thoughts when I found myself surrounded inexplicably by a dozen or so individuals. I had not seen them come and was taken by surprise. They were dressed in work clothes—jeans and work shirts—and two of them wore hard hats. Two others were sitting on machinery, and they were all watching me.

As if in response to my sad and perplexed heart—both at this startling event and my life in general at that time—an African-American gentleman, who was some distance ahead of me, turned and began walking toward me. His eyes were filled with tears and flowing with the love of God. I felt instant peace. I knew that he was an angel; he emanated the love of God.

God's divine love made an impact on my heart in those moments. Even today, I can draw on this memory and receive His love because of this angel's impartation into my life. I can draw from God's reservoir when my spiritual bank account of love feels depleted.

Regarding this and other supernatural experiences, I love what Job said to God: "I have heard of thee by the hearing of the ear, but now mine eye seeth thee" (Job 42:5 KJV). Everything that I saw in those few minutes looked physical, but maybe God gave me a vision and I was inside it, cooperating, and actively becoming a part of it. As I continued down the road, I sensed that all the "men" had disappeared, but I did not look back. I did not even think of looking back, but wish that I had!

I thought later of the story of Jesus being transfigured before the three disciples on the mountain. The disciples saw Moses and Elijah and recognized them immediately. That is a miracle to me. How did they know them? Then, when Jesus alone stood before them, He told them not to relate the vision to anyone until He had risen from the dead. It seems likely that the disciples thought they were in a normal physical setting as they stood at the top of the mountain, but Jesus called it a vision.

So was this experience along the road a vision or was it real? It seemed normal, and God did it for His glory, so I leave it at that.

One word of caution as I close this chapter on angels. I am reminded of the words of the apostle John in the book of Revelation:

> Now I, John, saw and heard these things. And when I heard and saw, I fell down to worship before the feet of the angel who showed me these things. Then he said to me, "See that you do not do that. For I am your fellow servant, and of your brethren the prophets, and of those who keep the words of this book. Worship God."
>
> Revelation 22:8–9

It is wonderful when God chooses in His mercy to send His angelic assistants—His messengers and helpers—but we must never worship angels. We must worship only God. Angels are "all ministering spirits sent forth to minister for those who will inherit salvation" (Hebrews 1:14 NKJV). Angels are real, but they are God's servants. He is so much greater.

We might not always understand the ways that God is working in the events of our lives, but we can know that

Jesus will be with us—that a touch from heaven is near. As we pray to Him, trusting Him, He will provide all of the supernatural help we need—angelic or otherwise—to navigate the challenges of our world and accomplish the work He has called us to do.

14

THE ABIDING PRESENCE
OF GOD

"But for you who fear my name, the Sun of Righteousness will rise with healing in his wings. And you will go free, leaping with joy like calves let out to pasture."

Malachi 4:2 NLT

The LORD was going before them in a pillar of cloud by day to lead them on the way, and in a pillar of fire by night to give them light, that they might travel by day and by night.

Exodus 13:21

At the end of eighteen months our work at Pensacola came to an end, and the Lord guided us forward once more. This time the Lord's direction came through the obvious. After Leonard's death, Martha decided to move to

Argentina to be near her oldest son and his family. We bought her home and prepared for life in Texas.

This was the last time I saw Martha. Her health degenerated, and she entered glory. David and I thanked God that, as our friend had prophesied, our parents had died in peace.

God had told me that my last day in our house in Pensacola would be special, and I was wondering what this might mean. He had asked me, *Why do you think I have left you alone, and away from people?* I pondered those words through the early morning hours as I prepared for the arrival of the trucks that would be moving our belongings. Perhaps He was going to give closure to the season of aloneness that I had experienced for so many months.

David was flying home that afternoon from Chicago. As soon as he arrived and the trucks left, we would head for Texas, driving both of our cars straight through the night.

No neighbors stirred in the early morning as I made yet another trip to the cars. My arms were full of pillows, blankets, food, plants as I went back and forth, packing perishable things or things that we would need right away when we arrived. A light mist, almost a drizzle, muted any sound.

Our cars were finally filled to overflowing; I could not squeeze in one more thing. I gave the car doors a final shove shut. The trucks would be arriving within the hour.

Our house was on a slope. Walking back up the incline of sidewalk I looked around and noticed that the mist had mostly dissipated. Then I glanced up.

What looked like a mushroom cloud—the shape we associate with the great power of an atomic bomb—was forming over our home. It seemed to be rising right out of the backyard. I considered how close it was but did not think to go and look. I stood transfixed.

It continued to rise, churning from below, getting larger from the bottom, being formed as I watched it. Then it took the shape of a man, with arms outstretched over the house and toward me. Creamy clouds hung down in drapes from the waist and sleeves like a robe.

I could hear something, too. There was a bit of a sound. Sometimes when I see unusual things happening I hear a noise in my ear. I cannot explain it. It is different—not an earthly sound.

The cloud continued to rise, and my eyes focused on a bit of movement on the rooftop. A small blackbird was perched there. It was silhouetted clearly in front of the brightness of the cloud. The bird, I knew, represented the feelings of rejection and isolation in me that I had struggled with for much of my life—that "lonely bird on a housetop."

And I realized that the cloud figure soaring above it was a clear picture of God's abiding presence and power.

At this point, the head of the cloud began to move to the left and the whole figure followed, dissipating into the sky.

As the billows began to separate and blow gently away, the arms looked as though they were reaching out. A message was impressed on my heart: *Follow the cloud because it is leaving today! You are going where I've led you. Do not be afraid.*

The blackbird took off, and I walked slowly up the sidewalk. What an astounding confirmation that God was leading us into the future!

Then in my heart I heard these words: *Blessed is he who believes in Me. Greater works shall he do because I go to the Father.*

I got my Bible—one of the few things not packed away—and found the reference in John 14:12 from which these words were paraphrased.

Then I sensed the Lord directing me to the beautiful words of Psalm 84:

> How lovely are Your dwelling places, O LORD of hosts! My soul longed and even yearned for the courts of the LORD; my heart and my flesh sing for joy to the living God. The bird also has found a house, and the swallow a nest for herself . . . even Your altars, O LORD of hosts. . . . How blessed are those who dwell in Your house! They are ever praising You. How blessed is the [one] whose strength is in You, in whose heart are the highways to Zion! Passing through the valley of Baca they make it a spring; the early rain also covers it with blessings. They go from strength to strength. . . . O LORD God of hosts, hear my prayer . . . and look upon the face of Your anointed. For a day in Your courts is better than a thousand outside. . . . For the LORD God is a sun and shield; the LORD gives grace and glory; no good thing does He withhold from those who walk uprightly. O LORD of hosts, how blessed is the [one] who trusts in You!

The presence of God came over that house. For some reason I did not understand I told the movers, who were Christians, about the cloud. As they filled the trucks with our belongings, they went about quietly, practically whispering. God was not only over the house, but in the house as well.

I was filled that day with the sense that we are vulnerable, but that God is all powerful. He comes alongside and enables us—and leads us on the path ahead.

After we had lived in Texas for about a year, David was speaking in North Carolina for the weekend and I was home alone passing a quiet evening in front of the television. Suddenly, deep in my heart, with the ears of my spirit, I heard the Lord say, *I am going to visit you.*

In a moment, I knew from somewhere within myself that the Lord was in the room. I turned my head and saw Him sitting on the sofa. He was wearing His long white robe.

His presence was physical. He was right there. When He comes like this, He looks as though one might—like the woman in the crowd—reach out and touch the hem of His robe if one wanted to. He is that real.

I saw Him for only a moment; He disappeared into thin air. But the picture is etched in my mind. His face was free of judgment and condemnation. He was pure innocence. I felt His love.

When I have had occasion to share my story, people always say: "I believe that if God can do this for you, He can do this for me." It seems right to me to pray that He will come to us visibly, or that He will open our eyes to see His ongoing supernatural power at work around us. He has told me more than once, *You know I answer prayer.*

I love the lines from the beautiful old hymn "Guide Me, O Thou Great Jehovah":

> Guide me, O Thou great Jehovah,
> Pilgrim through this barren land;
> I am weak, but Thou art mighty;
> Hold me with Thy powerful hand;
> Bread of heaven, Bread of heaven,
> Feed me till I want no more,
> Feed me till I want no more.

Open now the crystal fountain,
Whence the healing stream doth flow;
Let the fire and cloudy pillar
Lead me all my journey through;
Strong Deliverer, strong Deliverer,
Be Thou still my strength and shield,
Be Thou still my strength and shield.

Although these words speak to our hearts' desire to be home with Him in heaven, I think that most of us want to sense His presence here on earth, too.

But that does not happen every day. I long for Him to come, but never know when He will appear. And when I need to know His will, often it is the mundane that guides me rather than His glorious presence or shimmering angels on the path He wants me to take. Sometimes the supernatural directions He gives are so easy and natural I could miss them.

But Jesus goes ahead of us. He knows the way. We can navigate the paradoxes and idiosyncrasies of life because we have that assurance.

David and I have learned that when Jesus calls us to follow Him, He will help us. Sometimes the journey is filled with mountains and valleys that are difficult to traverse—but then He guides us on the path ahead.

The Lord showed me an unusual picture once. I was sitting on the beach alone, when a vision seemed to come down through the sky toward me.

It was a beautiful valley with long dark green grass and rough pink rocks along the hillside and pathways. A bubbling stream rushed down the hillside, and the sun shone brightly. I felt as if the vision came down upon me, encapsulating me.

I cried out to the Lord as I sat there, "Lord, where am I?"

Nancy, you're in the valley of the shadow of death.

"Lord, I didn't know it was so beautiful in this valley!"

I sat there amazed. Then the vision was lifted back up into the sky.

What did this mean?

Jesus promises to lead us out of darkness into His light so that we might proclaim His praises: "But you are a chosen generation, a royal priesthood, a holy nation, His own special people, that you may proclaim the praises of Him who called you out of darkness into His marvelous light" (1 Peter 2:9 NKJV).

Maybe you are in a difficult or challenging place right now. Maybe you need to know that Jesus will light even the darkest valley with His peace and beauty and lead you on. If so, fasten your eyes on Jesus and believe in your heart that help is near as you read His Word, pray and walk with Him by faith. The Lord is real and He is alive.

As you become more attuned to the occurrences around you, I think that you will be surprised at how many "coincidences" are really supernatural events happening at their appointed times. I know that if He allows me to experience these supernatural things, then He can do the same for you.

Look at these wonderful promises from Scripture:

He is the Father of lights, with whom there is no variation or shadow of turning (see James 1:17).

He remains the same yesterday, today and forever (see Hebrews 13:8).

He said of Himself, "I am the Lord, and I do not change" (see Malachi 3:6).

His delight is in His children (see Proverbs 8:31).

He loves you with an everlasting love (see Jeremiah 31:3). He will never leave you or forsake you (see Hebrews 13:5).

Jesus Christ is our Shepherd, Friend, Father, Savior, Provider and Deliverer. It is wonderful to know that He meets our needs supernaturally, but we need to be careful not to limit Him as to how He chooses to do this. Sometimes He will overwhelm us with His comforting presence, while at other times He might convict us. One moment He might discipline us, and another delight us, challenge us or caress us. He might speak to us audibly or circumstantially, through His Word or through the word of a friend or stranger.

But regardless of how He chooses to work in our lives, it is always to do good for us in the end (see Deuteronomy 8:16).

It is my sincere prayer that my personal encounters with the God of heaven will encourage you and build your faith to believe that no matter what you are going through, God is greater than your circumstances. Turn and look to Him, for He is the answer to every need and longing, every fear and failure, every difficulty or despair, every sin or sorrow.

Then as you look up and see Jesus with the eyes of faith, you will know—truly know—that you have been touched by heaven.

EPILOGUE

David Ravenhill

Saint Patrick is credited with saying, "If you try to explain the Trinity, you will lose your mind; but if you deny the Trinity you will lose your soul."

No one is capable of fully explaining God. How can we mere mortals explain The Immortal? And yet many have tried to do exactly that. In doing so, we have reduced God to the limits of our own understanding. J. B. Phillips, who gave us the Phillips' translation of the New Testament, wrote a book titled *Your God Is Too Small*. This is the end result of man trying to explain God; he ends up with a god no different from himself.

Nowhere is this more evident than when man attempts to explain the supernatural. The majority of Christians know better than to tamper with God's Word, and so reluctantly embrace the fact that the Bible contains scores of supernatural and unexplainable events in the four thousand years of human history that it records. When it comes to the *present*, however, we quickly seek to distance ourselves from the belief that God can do these things today.

In seeking to explain why, we fall prey immediately to the belief that God has chosen to cease any and all supernatural activity during this present age. This falls under the teaching of dispensationalism, which many Christians believe and adhere to. They have written God a doctrinal "tardy note" and exempted Him from performing any supernatural activity while they are in charge.

Another way to look at this is to place God in a theological straitjacket in which He is restrained from being Himself. What is so paradoxical is that these same believers will join with the choir in singing that Jesus is the same, yesterday, today and forever.

Rather than blaming our own unbelief in the supernatural, we place the blame on God's shoulders. Jesus Himself ran into this problem. We are told that He could do no mighty works in His hometown because of *their* unbelief. It was unbelief that kept Israel wandering around the wilderness for forty years—all due to the fact that they heeded the voice of their fellowmen rather than the voice of the living God. There is little doubt that God would have fulfilled His word to them, if they had not chosen instead to listen to the voices of eight of the ten spies.

Unbelief is one of the greatest obstacles—if not *the* greatest—to the operation and manifestation of the supernatural. Paul, writing to the Corinthians, tells us that the natural man does not accept the things of the Spirit because they seem like foolishness to him. Because these things defy reason, we reject them. The carnal mind, we are told, is an enemy of God. Paul in giving his defense before King Agrippa said,

"Why is it considered incredible among you people if God does raise the dead?" (Acts 26:8). The disciples themselves battled with unbelief. They had witnessed firsthand the raising of Lazarus and the widow of Nain's son, yet they failed to believe Jesus would rise from the tomb.

Thankfully, there are still some who believe that God has "no variableness, neither shadow of turning" (James 1:17 KJV), and remains "able to do exceeding abundantly above all we ask or think" (Ephesians 3:20 KJV).

Jesus, you recall, told His disciples prior to leaving them that they would do greater works than those He did because He was going to the Father (see John 14:12). Somehow our modern-day Sadducees (the Sadducees did not believe in the supernatural) have managed to change that to: "Now that I'm leaving you and returning to the Father, I'm no longer going to be doing any more mighty works." There is absolutely no scriptural evidence pointing to an end to all supernatural activity.

Rather, the opposite is true as proven by the book of Acts or, more accurately, *The Acts of the Apostles.* The Early Church continued the ministry that our Lord began. Following the Day of Pentecost they gathered to pray: "Grant that Your bondservants may speak Your word with all confidence, while You extend Your hand to heal, *and* signs and wonders take place through the name of Your holy servant Jesus" (Acts 4:29–30, italics added).

There is no doubt from their prayer that they fully expected to see the supernatural activity of the Holy Spirit confirm the word they preached. That is why we have "The Acts of the Apostles" and not "The Words of the Apostles."

One major aspect of the supernatural that is often overlooked is that it reveals the *glory* of God. By the glory of

God, I am referring to the nature and character of God. When Moses cried out to the Lord, "Show me Thy glory," the Lord told Moses that He was going to proclaim the name of the Lord to him. God is revealed to us by His name, nature or character. Moses was then told to stand on the rock. (The rock was a type of Christ.) As Moses was hidden in the cleft of the rock, the Lord passed by revealing His glory or character.

Jesus in His High Priestly Prayer (see John 17) declared, "I glorified You on the earth" (verse 4). He went on to say, "I have manifested Your name" (verse 6). The glory of God and the name of God are inseparable. When Jesus performed His first miracle by turning water into wine at the wedding in Cana of Galilee, John records: "This beginning of His signs Jesus did in Cana of Galilee, and manifested His *glory*" (John 2:11, italics added). The miraculous or supernatural manifestations are just as much a part of God's nature and character as His love, justice and holiness. When we fail to recognize the supernatural, we diminish the very nature and character of God Himself.

The apostle Paul in his first letter to the Corinthian believers reminds them that prior to turning in faith to God they were idol worshipers (see 1 Corinthians 12:1–3). What is interesting in his letter is the fact that he states: "You were led astray to the mute idols" (verse 2). Here he reminds them of the fact that their gods never spoke; they were mute. He goes on to tell them in the very next sentence that the Spirit of God *speaks*. It is this contrast that sets God apart from the gods of the nations. The remaining chapter deals with how God speaks. He reveals His wisdom through a word of wisdom, His knowledge through a word of knowledge, etc. One of the tragic results of those who teach that God no longer *speaks* is that we are now left with a *mute* God; one who is little different from the idols of heathenism.

When the early disciples prayed that the Lord would extend His hand to heal, they understood that the miraculous validated their message and that God could heal not only the body but also the soul. Paul, likewise, in his letter to the Corinthians encouraged the Church to "desire earnestly spiritual gifts" (1 Corinthians 14:1).

I believe that *our* failure to desire earnestly spiritual gifts has resulted in the absence of the gifts being in operation in the Church today. Not only have we grown accustomed to not seeing the gifts in operation, but we have been warned by many of our leading theologians and teachers that we no longer need these gifts. Their reasoning goes like this: God gave the gifts initially to "jump start" His Church, but once the Church was established, He then withdrew them. This reasoning is ridiculous. It is like saying that money is first minted in order to establish a nation's economy, but once its economy is operational, its currency can be removed. Or that the alphabet was first given in order to establish a new language, but now that we are conversant with the language the alphabet is no longer necessary. What type of logic is that?

Jesus warned the scribes and Pharisees about shutting off the Kingdom of heaven from people (see Matthew 23:13). The Bible defines the Kingdom as not just words but power. Jesus said, "If I cast out demons by the Spirit of God, then the kingdom of God has come upon you" (Matthew 12:28). Today we are witnessing in the Church these same "scribes and Pharisees" shutting off the power of God's Kingdom by teaching that His power has currently been placed on hold. If as believers we heed Jesus' admonition to pray *Thy Kingdom come*, then we should honestly expect to see a demonstration of His Kingdom power in our midst.

Speaking of demons, I would like to know from those who teach that the gifts have been withdrawn if they also believe that the devil has withdrawn his demonic hordes and lost his power also. One of the nine gifts of the Holy Spirit was discerning of spirits. If Satan and his hosts of darkness are still around, then he must be jubilant to know that Christians no longer have the ability to discern between evil spirits and the work of the Holy Spirit.

This leads me to another tactic of the devil. If he can deceive us into believing that all supernatural activity has ceased, then he can move about unhindered and unopposed. I have always been fascinated by the account of the Philistines in their relentless war against God's people, Israel. On this occasion they succeeded in eliminating every blacksmith shop in Israel. How long this took we are not told; neither do we know how they did it. This resulted in the Israelites having to go to the Philistines every time they broke one of their agricultural implements, whether it was a fork, hoe, plow or axe. The Philistines levied a charge for repairing every item, and in this way made God's people dependent upon their archenemy.

Israel, however, while inconvenienced by this, was blind-sided by the Philistines' real objective in eliminating their blacksmiths. It was the blacksmiths who made not only the agricultural implements but also the weapons of war. This resulted in Israel being totally powerless on the day of battle. So much so that only the king and his son had weapons with which to fight (see 1 Samuel 13:19–23). I am fully convinced that the greater Philistine, the devil, concocted a diabolical plan to deceive the Church into believing that the very gifts that God gave us to use for the advancement of His Kingdom are no longer available today. Sadly, the end result of all of this aberrant teaching has been to diminish the Church's power while reinforcing the power of the enemy.

My father, Leonard Ravenhill, said often that psychology and psychiatry are man's substitutes for the gifts of the Holy Spirit. I have witnessed personally the impact a "word of knowledge" can have on an individual by revealing the root to some spiritual blockage in his or her life. A great biblical example of this was when Jesus told the woman at the well that she was currently living with a man as well as having had five previous husbands. These spiritual gifts were given as "tools for the trade." If you take away someone's tools, he is going to be greatly limited in his ability to accomplish the task he sets out to do.

Can you see how the enemy must delight in this? He becomes more powerful and we become less effective. Why, we must ask ourselves, would God remove His power from His Church and thereby give the enemy the upper hand?

In my fifty years of ministry around the globe, I have seen and experienced firsthand the operation of the gifts of the Holy Spirit. I can find not one single scriptural reference to them ever being cancelled or withdrawn. I might not always have the answer as to why some get healed and some do not; nor do I fully understand why we do not see and experience more supernatural activity than we do. But, as Nancy has mentioned in her story, we often quote my late father as saying: "A man or a woman with an experience is never at the mercy of a man or a woman with an argument." I have tasted and I have seen!

There are three major reasons that I believe the supernatural is for today.

Biblical evidence
Historical evidence
Personal evidence

Allow me to elaborate briefly on these points.

First of all *biblically*. Any casual reader of the Bible has to conclude that from Genesis to Revelation the Bible is filled with the supernatural activity of God. Who can begin to fathom how God was able to speak Creation into being, not to mention the infinite variety of birds, animals, insects, vegetation and trees that He also created? We can look up any evening into the starry heavens and marvel at God's amazing handiwork, or delve into the oceans and view the vast variety of fish with their camouflage of size and color. Yes, almost every page of God's Word reveals His mighty power and awesome acts.

Historically, we can trace God's supernatural power throughout the ages. Virtually every generation of believers from the New Testament to the present has seen the evidence of God's miraculous power. Regarding his thoroughly researched and documented book *Miracles and Manifestations of the Holy Spirit in the History of the Church*, author Jeff Doles states:

> *God has always done miracles in His Church—and still does!* The Holy Spirit has never left the Church and neither have His supernatural gifts and manifestations. They have been available in every century—from the days of the Apostolic Fathers, to the desert monks of Egypt and Syria, to the missionary outreaches of the Middle Ages, to the Reformation

era and the awakenings and revivals that followed, to the Pentecostal explosion of the Twentieth Century and the increase of signs and wonders in the Twenty-first. Miracles, healings, deliverances, prophecies, dreams, visions—even raising the dead!—have all been in operation throughout the history of the Church. Anglicans, Baptists, Catholics, Congregationalists, Lutherans, Methodists, Moravians, Presbyterians, Quakers and many others have experienced the supernatural gifts and workings of the Spirit over the centuries.

Personally, I have witnessed the supernatural in my own life. I was raised in a godly Christian home, the middle son of three. My two brothers were extremely gifted academically and always seemed to rise to the top in their respective classes.

I was the least gifted and struggled through most of my school years. On more than one occasion, I brought home *F*s on my report card. My years in Bible school were not much better. Adding to my academic ineptitude, I was extremely shy and reluctant to promote myself in any way. My homiletics teacher told me that I was one of the shyest and most nervous students he had ever taught.

Following our marriage, Nancy and I began our ministry at Teen Challenge in Brooklyn, New York, with David Wilkerson, as she has described. My father had met a man who moved in the realm of the Holy Spirit and invited him to speak to a number of the Teen Challenge staff one evening. Following a time of sharing we had a season of prayer. I was kneeling beside a chair in the corner of the room with my face buried in my hands. My only prayer that evening was an internal cry for wisdom. My lips were not moving and no sound was coming out of my mouth. Within thirty seconds of my prayer, I felt hands being placed on my head and the man said to me, "God has heard your cry for wisdom and has given it to you."

Needless to say, I was overwhelmed and began to cry. He went on to say, "I'm having a vision of you. I see you standing and speaking into a microphone before hundreds and hundreds of brown-skinned people who are sitting in a large field." Then he told me that I would stand before kings and rulers.

My first reaction was one of total disbelief. How could God use me? I had no ability to speak whatsoever, let alone speak before kings. My native England had a ruling Queen, but at that moment I was struggling to think of any country with a king.

Within three years, every word of that prophetic vision had come to pass. I was one of the leaders from New Zealand who went with a Youth With A Mission team to the small island nation of Tonga. Several leaders were asked by the Methodist church to speak at their Sunday afternoon open-air gathering in the city of Nukualofa, the capital city in Tonga.

The third week we were there, I was asked to speak. Due to the coronation of the king that coming week, the venue was changed to a large park just beside the king's palace. As I stood to speak I looked out on hundreds and hundreds of brown-skinned Polynesian people. I was facing away from the king's palace as I spoke to them, unaware of what was going on behind me. Following my message I was surrounded by various team members informing me that as I spoke, the king stood on the balcony, listening to me.

I recalled immediately the prophetic word three years earlier. Never could I have engineered such a set of circumstances even if I had tried. It proved to me that God is still in the business of the supernatural.

When we are dealing with the supernatural we cannot limit God in any way. Paul states in his letter to the Corinthians that there are "varieties of gifts . . . varieties of ministries . . . varieties of effects, but the same God who works all things in all persons" (1 Corinthians 12:4–6).

This is revealed to us in the word that God spoke to Aaron and Miriam:

> "Hear now My words: If there is a prophet among you, I, the LORD, shall make Myself known to him in a vision. I shall speak to him in a dream. Not so, with My servant Moses, He is faithful in all My household; with him I speak mouth to mouth, even openly, and not in dark sayings, and he beholds the form of the LORD."
>
> Numbers 12:6–8

In these verses we see a variety of ways that the Lord can communicate with His people. This is true not only throughout the Old Testament, but also throughout the New Testament. Mary and Joseph had dreams and visions, as did Peter and Paul. Angels were another way God communicated to His people. God also spoke through the gift of tongues and interpretation, as well as the gift of prophecy. He revealed His wisdom through words of wisdom and His knowledge through words of knowledge. None of these avenues of communication should ever differ from or contradict the written Word of God, for as Scripture says: "Thou hast magnified thy word above all thy name" (Psalm 138:2 KJV).

As with any supernatural activity, we should never focus on the person or the event but rather on the Lord Himself. If any of these unusual activities draws attention away from the supremacy and centrality of Christ, then we must seriously question its validity. We are told in Revelation 19:10 that "the testimony of Jesus is the spirit of prophecy." In other words, everything should ultimately exalt and magnify the Lord Jesus Christ. This, you recall, was the work Jesus said the Holy Spirit was sent to do: "He will glorify Me, for He will take of Mine and will disclose it to you" (John 16:14).

The question is often asked: Why do these things happen to certain individuals and not to the likes of me? There are a variety of answers to that vital question.

First of all, we are told in Romans 9:21: "Does not the potter have a right over the clay, to make from the same lump one vessel for honorable use and another for common use?" While God is no respecter of persons, He does have the right to do as He wills.

Secondly, the gifts are given severally as He wills. This does not mean that if you are lacking in this area you are any less important. Just as the physical body is composed of many members, each having its specific function, so also is the Body of Christ, the Church. We each have our own unique gifts and callings.

Thirdly, having understood that, we are encouraged to desire earnestly spiritual gifts. In other words, these gifts are available to those who really desire them for His glory.

Finally, I believe we can insult the Spirit of God by our unbelief and thereby "limit the holy One of Israel." Jesus reprimanded the Pharisees for shutting off the Kingdom of God from people: "But woe to you, scribes and Pharisees, hypocrites, because you shut off the kingdom of heaven from people; for you do not enter in yourselves, nor do you allow those who are entering to go in" (Matthew 23:13). This verse reveals the tremendous influence spiritual leaders have over those under them. They can teach that the gifts of the Holy Spirit are no longer for today and, thereby, turn an entire church or denomination against seeking after them.

Even if you are doubtful and have been taught that God no longer chooses to operate in the supernatural realm, remember that in the last days we will see God doing amazing demonstrations of power, as described throughout the book of Revelation. He will give power to His two witnesses to prophesy and do miracles, for instance.

I choose to believe that God has never withheld or withdrawn His power and remains the same today as He was yesterday, and will be forevermore.

The supernatural God.

Nancy Ravenhill and her husband, David, both graduates of Bethany Bible College in Bloomington, Minnesota, have served together in ministry since their marriage in 1964. They first joined Teen Challenge in New York City and then ministered in the South Pacific with Youth With A Mission. They made their home in Christchurch, New Zealand, where David was on the pastoral team of one of New Zealand's largest churches, The New Life Centre. After returning to the United States, they pastored as part of the Kansas City Fellowship, and then pastored a Vineyard Church in Washington State. Now residents of Siloam Springs, Arkansas, they serve as itinerate ministers, taking the Gospel all over the world as the Lord calls them. The Ravenhills have three daughters and eight grandchildren.

Available from Leonard Ravenhill

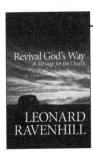